The Black Hole

The Black Hole

Money, Myth and Empire

JAN DALLEY

PENGUIN
FIG TREE

For my father

FIG TREE

Published by the Penguin Group
Penguin Books Ltd, 80 Strand, London WC2R ORL, England
Penguin Group (USA) Inc., 375 Hudson Street, New York, New York 10014, USA
Penguin Group (Canada), 90 Eglinton Avenue East, Suite 700, Toronto, Ontario, Canada M4P 2Y3
(a division of Pearson Penguin Canada Inc.)
Penguin Ireland, 25 St Stephen's Green, Dublin 2, Ireland (a division of Penguin Books Ltd)
Penguin Group (Australia), 250 Camberwell Road,
Camberwell, Victoria 3124, Australia (a division of Pearson Australia Group Pty Ltd)
Penguin Books India Pvt Ltd, 11 Community Centre,
Panchsheel Park, New Delhi – 110 017, India
Penguin Group (NZ), cnr Airborne and Rosedale Roads, Albany,
Auckland 1310, New Zealand (a division of Pearson New Zealand Ltd)
Penguin Books (South Africa) (Pty) Ltd, 24 Sturdee Avenue,
Rosebank, Johannesburg 2196, South Africa

Penguin Books Ltd, Registered Offices: 80 Strand, London WC2R ORL, England

www.penguin.com

First published 2006
1

Set in 12/14.75 pt Monotype Bembo
Typeset by Rowland Phototypesetting Ltd, Bury St Edmunds, Suffolk
Printed in Great Britain by Clays Ltd, St Ives plc

A CIP catalogue record for this book is available from the British Library

HARDBACK
ISBN-13: 978–0–670–91447–0
ISBN-10: 0–670–91447–9

Contents

List of Illustrations

Every effort has been made to trace copyright holders. The publishers will be glad to rectify in future editions any errors or omissions brought to their attention.

Acknowledgements

Andrew Motion gave me the idea for this book, and persuaded me to write it; Sunil Khilnani gave me inspiration and hospitality; and Roy Foster and David Gilmour both gave me generous advice, encouragement and essential history lessons. I'm also grateful to several other friends, in Britain and in Calcutta, for their support and kindness. The staff of the India Office Collection at the British Library and the staff of the London Library were unfailingly helpful, and my warm thanks go to my editors at Fig Tree, Juliet Annan and Carly Cook, and to my copy-editor David Watson, as well as to my agent Carol Heaton, for their help and their patience.

A Note on Place-Names

Throughout this book I refer to the cities of India as Calcutta, Bombay and Madras instead of by their modern appellations, Kolkata, Mumbai and Chennai. This is because I decided to adopt a single standardized English usage for all places and nationalities, and so I refer to the Dutch, the French, the Danes, the Portuguese and so on instead of using their own national terms. It is also for consistency and clarity – to refer to eighteenth-century Calcutta in the same sentence as modern-day Kolkata would be cumbersome and confusing. Similarly, I have standardized the transliteration of Indian names for the sake of consistency and clarity.

Preface

We read history to find out more about ourselves. The narratives of the past are like a national or cultural family album, full of pictures and stories that give us a sense of the group to which we belong. In their psychological effect on us, it may hardly matter whether the stories are momentous or trivial – the day the wasp stung Granny on a picnic may be as powerful, in our personal mythology, as the more distant knowledge of a vast battle won or the great tragic movements of a whole people through starvation or slavery or war. Without such stories, large and small, we do not know who we are.

This book is about a story that entered the national mythbank of the British people and lodged there with unusual tenacity. There must have been something about it that the British needed. As so often with the historical episodes the British take to their hearts, it is a story of heroism in failure, one that could somehow turn a miserable defeat into a matter of national pride. There was something special, it seems, in this tale, in the romance of hearing about a few brave countrymen, far away on the edge of a mysterious continent, battling against great forces and losing their lives on the whim of an imperious tyrant – or perhaps through a sorry blunder.

The story of the Black Hole of Calcutta was, in outline, as follows. In 1756, the town of Calcutta was a medium-sized trading settlement, established a few decades earlier by the British East India Company and growing rapidly into the most important and profitable of their commercial settlements. An apparently imposing fort stood above the busy river, and a small European contingent of merchants and their families employed a huge web of local people: Calcutta's 'Black Town' already contained hundreds of thousands.

The local nawab, the representative of the Mughal court centred in Delhi, was Siraj-ud-daulah, a young hothead who had recently inherited the throne from his wiser grandfather, Alivardi. Siraj was not interested in continuing the mutually advantageous balance of trade and power that existed between the Mughal rulers and all the European traders in the area – there were French, Dutch, Portuguese and others – and disliked especially what he saw as the arrogant behaviour of the British. Sabre-rattling and skirmishes between the Europeans and the Indians were not uncommon, but this was different: Siraj was determined to drive the foreigners out of his country. Within weeks of taking the throne, he marched on Calcutta with a huge army; the British could only muster a defensive force of 515 men. After a fierce battle lasting several days, the British were beaten. The nawab's soldiers took possession of the fort, and that first night – 20 June 1756 – the remaining defenders were locked up in a small cell, to await the nawab's pleasure the next day.

According to the school-book version that was current in Britain for two centuries, 146 people were locked into a room that measured 14 ft by 18 ft, and had only two small, high, barred windows for air. The monsoon was late coming that year, so it must have been one of the hottest nights of that sweltering place. When the door was opened in the morning, all but twenty-three had died, horribly, of crushing, suffocation and thirst.

Almost since the first reports of the story, its veracity has been questioned. Apart from anything else, it is generally agreed to have been physically impossible to put so many people in a space of that size. And even those who believed the official version of the facts disputed the nawab's intentions:

was it deliberate brutality on the part of the victor, or was it simply a sad mistake on the part of his soldiers?

The durability of the doubts about the incident seemed not to impede its power and usefulness as a national legend. The story was used for good and for ill. All tales of human bravery and resilience have an important place in our minds, and this one came with other attractive characteristics: the aura of money and battles, of exotic places and people, of youth and daring and living against the odds. There is probably no great harm if a little exaggeration creeps in to such narratives. However, the way in which this particular episode also resonated as a fear of strangeness, and came to epitomize through its very name the savagery of other peoples, is much less savoury.

Because of this, the accuracy of the story begins to matter more than it otherwise would. In the nation's mythology (as opposed to the stricter annals of properly disinterested history) it can hardly matter if the details of, say, the Charge of the Light Brigade were a little fudged by Tennyson, if he made the 'six hundred' into tragic heroes when another account might have written them up as disorganized dupes. It would only matter if the revised version became something that influenced our view of Turkish or Russian artillery or Cossack horsemen, to their detriment, in some future balance of power.

The Black Hole of Calcutta was never, to my knowledge, specifically quoted as a reason for the British to take one course of action or another in India. But when Robert Clive marched on Calcutta to recapture the Company's possessions, he seized the opportunity to take two decisive steps in the direction of full colonial power. He made a deal with a more amenable contender for the throne of Bengal – Mir Jaffir, a kinsman of Siraj – and thereby changed the balance of power inexorably. While Siraj had been a fiery and independent spirit, Mir Jaffir was all but a puppet ruler. Clive also used the fact that Britain was by now at war with France in Europe to take possession of some of the French settlements and territories, which in effect meant a partial territorial conquest of Bengal itself. Although the East India Company had always claimed that it had no interest in acquiring land in India, this was exactly what came about.

Even more importantly, perhaps, the Black Hole incident became one of those iconic happenings in the collective national memory around which national sentiment crystallizes, and which – consciously or unconsciously – license certain sorts of retaliatory behaviour.

The received version of the Black Hole incident was clearly flawed. It didn't have a Tennyson as its apologist, only a more prosaic balladeer in the chief survivor, John Zephaniah Holwell, who had to save his own neck with his employers once he had escaped his captors. His account has been challenged since the day it was published and continues even now, among those who still know anything about it, to arouse controversy. Although we will never know the exact truth, because the evidence just isn't there – perhaps even precisely because we will never know the exact truth – all the exaggerations and distortions, the small mendacities and the larger generalizations, take on a greater significance.

These contradictions and inaccuracies are the subject of the book. The way stories are told gives us so much information about what the story means to the teller, and it's there the interest lies. The night of the Black Hole, in June 1756, can be seen as one small event among the many miseries of a war-torn century, not a particularly great or significant one, a rather pointless loss of life through a series of mistakes. Alternatively, that night can be seen as a turning point, a moment at which the relationship between the British and the Indians, a commercial relationship based solely on mutual interest, began to shift inexorably towards control and empire.

One who believed this was Lord Curzon, Viceroy of India from 1899, who by an enthusiastic remaking of the Black Hole memorial rekindled the power of a myth that had already become lukewarm. If it had not been for Curzon, we might never have heard of the Black Hole of Calcutta. He believed it was a pivotal moment. He was in no doubt about its significance, and its direct relationship to the creation of the Raj: with his characteristic eloquence, he described the Black Hole victims as 'men whose life-blood cemented the foundations of the British Empire in India'.

When I was seven, I trotted off to school every day at a French convent in Tehran, where my parents lived at the time. I learnt very little, except the inalienable truth that the English were damned to perdition for burning Joan of Arc, and I did come away with a vague recollection of some story about the dashing Chasseurs d'Afrique, about the Fedioukine Hills and a general called D'Allonville. It was confused but heroic: definitely a tale of *la gloire*. I'd be embarrassed to admit how many years it was before I made any connection in my mind between this story and another, one that featured people called Lucan and Cardigan, and the 13th Light Dragoons riding up a narrow valley with 'cannon to right of them, cannon to left of them' – and realized that the two apparently separate stories were nothing but different nations' descriptions of the same incident during the Crimean War, the one the British know as the Charge of the Light Brigade. It was an unforgettable lesson in the malleability of historical information. Facts are facts, but they can be edited into a variety of shapes: what matters is how the story is told.

Perhaps it was this early experience of the relationship between historical truth and personal perspective that made me become fascinated with the Black Hole story, one of history's enduring puzzles. Like many more ancient legends, it only makes sense if the reader decides to suspend his disbelief – and it's part of the interest that many highly intelligent people have done just that, while so many others have pointed relentlessly to the factual discrepancies.

The other attraction was the identification I felt with the dramatis personae. The eighteenth-century employees of the East India Company were not colonists, or the servants of an overtly colonial power; they were traders who had come to a foreign place for the commercial exploitation of its resources rather than the domination or administration of its people – although of course that immediately begs all the interesting questions in the story, and in history's subsequent develop-ments. My father was a twentieth-century employee of a huge trading company, living in a foreign place for the commercial exploitation of its resources: my earliest memories are of life in a standard-issue company bungalow on a small oilfield in the desert of southern Iran. The employees of BP were hardly like the East India Company men of the 1750s – we had aeroplanes and vaccinations and swimming-pools; we had wonderful Iranian friends and we were never in danger of marauding nawabs.

I had no idea what it must have felt like, in the eighteenth century, to be in a strange place a year's perilous journey from home, in a climate that took a terrible death-toll on Europeans. But some things I did know. I knew what it was like trying to fall asleep on sweltering nights, my ears blocked in terror against the hideous yelps of hyena and jackal around the house. What it was like to live with intense heat, in the days before air-conditioning was everywhere: school from 5 a.m. to 10 a.m. in the summer; then a long, strange, dreamy middle of day in a shaded, silent house, before my father went back to work for several hours in the early evening. New shoes: standing squealing and giggly-ticklish on a big sheet of paper on the dining-room table as my mother drew around our bare toes, before the tracing was sent off to a London store that took so long to send back the dumpy Clark's sandals my father had to get out his penknife and cut the front off the shoes as soon as they arrived: they were already too small. The smell of chapattis, as one of Georgie's wives squatted at the brazier in the yard behind the kitchen, her bracelets clanking, fanning the coals and crooning to herself, slapping at our little legs with her flyswat when we tried to steal a taste before they were ready. Georgie, an ancient giant of a man who reigned in the kitchen, sliced and stirred with incredible speed given that he only had a few fingers on each hand – when we asked him what had happened to them, he'd grin roguishly and make a chopping movement over his own hand: 'Naughty!'

This sort of thing, you might think, is typical of any childhood spent in another land. Yet I have never felt the slightest affinity with the children of empire in their verandah'd bungalows, with their ayahs and their memsahib mothers and their fathers busy making the trains run through the Empire. It just wasn't like that for us. So when I started to read about the adventurers of the East India Company, I felt I knew much more about them, and what they were doing there. They didn't have a notion of service, as the officers of the Raj did. Their aim was to change their lives – my own father used to say that he'd first gone to the Middle East in the early 1950s to escape the drabness of post-war Britain as much as to earn a far better living than he would have done at home. And I felt I understood how these people lived in several worlds at once, as we did. Contrasting images that stay with me – a Persian wedding party at the house of our family doctor and my father's great friend, Abdy Hooseinpoor, for which a female sturgeon as big as a child's corpse had been brought packed in straw and ice all the way from the Caspian, so heavy it needed three men to lift it on to its own long table, where it lay in a slithery grey-black bumpy sea of its own caviar (I used to stare at the glistening mounds of this stuff, so like the shiny-slimy grey-black oil that governed our lives: both inexplicably valuable, inexplicably interesting to grown-ups). Then, and to me at five far more wonderful, discovering for the first time ready-made mayonnaise and sliced white bread in the huge American refrigerator of my best friend, Janet Joyce James, who wore pedal-pushers and two-tone brown and white lace-up shoes that I coveted passionately. These things were the true exotica.

If anyone had suggested to my parents that they were empire-builders, they would have been horrified. The retired relics of empire, with their uneasy nostalgia and their brass knick-knacks, belonged to their parents' world, not their own. Although the situation of the oil companies in pre-Khomeini Iran was thoroughly political, and the Shah played a crafty game in balancing the demands of the Americans and British who had put him on the throne against the might of the Soviet Union pushing at his northern borders, these were modern politics, not those of empire. It may have been the Cold War by another name, but it was nothing to do with the hot battles of imperial conquest.

But were they right, my parents? Or were they just avoiding a truth they did not like: that commercial intervention in a country cannot be without political consequences? In the last few years I've come to think that I was a child of empire, after all. It was not the empire of Great Britain, nor of any place that liked to use that word, but since September 11th the notion of the American empire has come into being like a slowly developing photograph, gaining clarity all the time: that's the one in which I lived. Looking back over the great arc of formal European imperialism, across two centuries, I see the men of the East India Company at the other side. They were determined not to be imperialists, either, but perhaps they already were. Lord Curzon believed so: he called them the 'unconscious builders of empire'. Like the oil empire in which I grew up, their hegemony of commerce was to have far-reaching effects for half the world.

1. The Mystery of Mary Carey

On 15 January 1754, early on a winter's day in Calcutta, Peter Carey – or perhaps Cary – a seaman who worked on one of the English ships that moved in and out of the Hooghly river in the service of the East India Company, married his sweetheart Mary. In the marriage register of St Anne's church, the only one in Calcutta at the time, she is described as a 'country woman'; after her Christian name, pathetically, eloquently, there is no surname. The page in the register is filled in the Reverend Gervase Bellamy's looping copperplate with a tightly packed parade of a dozen or more seamen and soldiers who that day married their Phoebes and Florences and Janes, most with no registered parentage or family name beyond the fact that they were a 'country woman' or 'of the country'. Unlike the vast majority of these nameless young women, and because of the random tides of history, Mary emerges from the crowd to appear in many later accounts: in one of these, too, she is described as 'a fine woman, tho' country born'.

That 'tho'' speaks volumes. What the expression means is not that Mary came from the country rather than the town, it meant that she was of the country, 'native' – probably, in this case, that she was the illegitimate child of an Indian mother by an unknown European father. Or perhaps, since we know from her later story that she was a Catholic, she might have been Maria, 'a Portugall', her family originally from Goa, where the early Portuguese settlement, and their deliberate policy of intermarriage and conversion, meant that there was already an established population of mixed parentage. As the British East India Company, along with the great merchant companies of the Netherlands and France, began to establish settlement-towns on the Indian continent, the Goans of Portuguese origin took an important role in the life of these fledgling cities, as soldiers or domestic servants, as facilitators, translators and much else, being as they were half in each world. But we don't know much about Mary: only that after her death she was buried in the Murgihatta (Portuguese Catholic) cathedral in Calcutta. A journalist who met and interviewed Mary when she was in her late fifties reported that she was 'of a fair Mesticia colour', and everyone agrees that she was very good-looking: the same account had her 'very well proportioned . . . with correct regular features, which give evident marks of beauty that must once have attracted admiration'.

But we will never know much more: the beautiful *mesticia* Mary or Maria was not the sort of person who would have had her portrait painted, although there was apparently an image that was supposed to be her, inside the painted lid of a trinket box kept by one of the family, somewhere, some time. Among the growing number of anonymous people whose short lives were lived in the backwash of exploration and colonization, belonging to neither world and both, not entirely welcome in either, young women like Mary could have made a marriage of relative ease to a young merchant, if they were lucky, but would more probably have led the harder life of the wife of a seaman or soldier, or become a domestic servant, or if they were very unlucky have joined the growing army of prostitutes for which Calcutta was already becoming notorious.

This Mary had a more unusual future. By the end of her life – she lived to be sixty, a good age in that place at that time – she had become famous as the only woman to survive the ordeal of the Black Hole of Calcutta, and the last of the survivors of that tragedy to die in India. Interviewed in 1799 by Thomas Boileau, an English journalist, she told him that she was then fifty-eight – which would have meant she was fifteen when she was incarcerated in the Black Hole, and thirteen at the time of her marriage. Were British seamen marrying thirteen-year-olds in the mid-eighteenth century? Would the good Reverend Bellamy have presided over such a match? Even allowing for a little latitude, however, she was obviously very young indeed.

Mary and Peter were cast in starring roles in the Black Hole drama of 1756 by the chief surviving witness, the man who shaped the history of the event, John Zephaniah Holwell, one of the East India Company's senior traders in Calcutta. In an account written the following year on board a homeward-bound ship, artfully framed in the form of a letter to a friend but certainly intended for publication, both Peter and Mary are vividly described in his highly coloured and emotional language – she tenderly cradling her young husband in her arms as he slowly and agonizingly expired from thirst and exhaustion, then emerging bravely from the hellish night, a 'fine' teenage widow, to meet a fate worse than death (Holwell hints darkly) in the harem of the local nawab. 'The rest who survived the fateful night regained their liberty [from the nawab's forces],' he writes, 'except Mrs Carey, who was too young and handsome.'

Did any of this happen? The strange thing is that in the first account of the tragedy Holwell wrote, in a letter dated 17 July 1756 – less than a month after the event itself – to his senior East India Company colleagues in Bombay and his employers, the Company's formidable board of directors in London, he makes no mention of either Peter or Mary Carey. He supplies a detailed list of those who died and those who survived: he names eight survivors, including himself, all British, all male. Apart from these named people, some of

3

whom were traders and 'Writers' (clerks) of the East India Company, some from among the few members of the militia who had not earlier deserted Fort William, Holwell says there were '7 or 8 soldiers, blacks and whites'. There is no woman among them, no Carey or Cary or even Carry on the list.

This letter, with other accounts of the tragedy – including, simultaneously, Holwell's own later and much revised version of events – arrived in London by ship a full eleven months after the happenings of 20 June, and the press grasped the story avidly. Reports in both Scotland and England go into considerable detail about names and numbers. In one of these, ostensibly quoting a letter from an (unnamed) eye-witness in Calcutta, the name 'Cary' appears in a list of eight 'seafaring men' reported killed in the battle to defend Calcutta against the invading forces of Siraj-ud-daulah, the nawab of Bengal – before the Black Hole incident took place. And the name 'Carey' is on a list of fifty European women, with their thirty-seven children, who were safely evacuated from the besieged Fort William in Calcutta and taken in a rickety ship down the river to sanctuary in the Dutch settlement at Fulta. So, according to this account, neither Peter nor Mary was among the Black Hole prisoners, alive or dead.

Here, in the accounts of important survivors and witnesses, and that of Mary Carey herself, apparently the only woman and the last to tell the tale, we get glimpses of inconsistencies and contradictions so elaborate that they will never be untangled. If literature has its artfully 'unreliable narrators', the history of this incident has a whole cast of unreliable survivors – possibly, in some cases, just as artful. Holwell may have had his reasons for massaging the statistics; Mary may have had her reasons for accepting a role that had not been hers. Indeed, she reverted to her Carey name even though she had quite soon after the Black Hole incident married again, an English 'military officer of field rank' called Weston, and had two sons and perhaps also a daughter with him. But when widowed a second time, she resumed the name of her more famous youth. What both these important and apparently unimpeachable commentators give us are examples of the way in which memories are edited, and then set, so that the narrator may believe his or her own version utterly, despite evidence to question it.

The uncertainties and ambiguities here are typical of the whole legend of the Black Hole of Calcutta, an incident whose resonance and fame would far outstrip its reality. And its reality, indeed, is something we shall never exactly know. Almost everything about the official account is now questioned, and has been challenged, even ridiculed, down the centuries. But that did not stop its enshrinement in British mythology, and especially the mythology of the British Empire in India. As one nineteenth-century historian put it, it was 'bitten into the national memory', and the bite sank deep.

A few things we do know. We know that on the night of 20 June 1756, the hottest night of the year because the late monsoon had not yet broken and the temperatures had climbed to extraordinary heights, even by the standards of that sultry place, a number of Indian, English, French, Dutch and Portuguese people were locked overnight into a small cell, the military prison of Calcutta's Fort William. It was known by the soldiery who used to sleep off their hangovers in it as the 'Black Hole'. It was at ground level, a walled-in section at the corner of the otherwise open arcade that ran around the central parade ground in the Fort; it was about 18 feet by 14; there were two small high grilles for air and a shelf along one side for sleeping on; it was meant to accommodate a handful of prisoners at most. Far from being some grim dungeon of the nawab's devising, it was the Englishmen's own prison.

In this tight and underventilated space, a number of those locked up by the soldiers of Siraj-ud-daulah, who had laid siege to the town for the past four days, died of thirst, or crushing, or suffocation – 'over-heat'd, and for want of water' as one contemporary account has it – or from the wounds they had received during the fierce battle for Calcutta that had raged for several days. That much we do know. They numbered 170, the unfortunate creatures in that hellish cell, and only sixteen came out alive, according to reports in the British press the following year, when the news arrived. Perhaps, though, some had been dead even before the door was slammed on them that night, because the Hole had been used as a repository for bodies during the course of the battle, when there was no way of burying them. Or else there were 175 who went in alive, and sixteen who survived, according to a contemporary letter from Calcutta. Or, perhaps – Holwell appended a postscript to his first letter of report, written a week or so later, although it arrived in London by the same ship – he had been mistaken about the number of prisoners in the Black Hole, and it had in fact been 146, of whom 123 had died.

These last figures, or something close to them, are the ones that were accepted and taught to generations of British schoolchildren. They became set in stone – literally, although a whole 145 years later – by the Viceory Lord Curzon, who in 1901 laid a dramatic black marble slab,

to mark the site of the prison in Old Fort William
known as the Black Hole
in which 146 British inhabitants of Calcutta
were confined on the night of the 20th June, 1756,
and from which only 23 came out alive

Subtly, almost imperceptibly, Curzon had here confirmed another layer to the myth, by recording that the 146 prisoners were 'British'. He may have meant that they were on the British side in the conflict – but he must have known perfectly well that they were not all British, nor even mostly British, because he had taken care to find out, and none of the early reporters had ever suggested that they were. But it did make a better story, and it was a story that stuck. From that date onwards, all commentators describe the prisoners as British. Yet of those twenty-three survivors, no one has ever been able to name more than a handful. Even Curzon, who recognized in the story of the Black Hole a potent tale of great importance to the imperial spirit, was hard put to identify even half the survivors, and to name only about a third of the supposed victims.

Yet he tried. The following year, in 1902, he erected his monument to the Black Hole victims – it was a marble replica of the monument that Holwell himself had raised, only a few years after the tragedy, but that first one had been of brick and had crumbled away by the 1820s, without apparently much regret on the part of the inhabitants of the newly burgeoning city. So mid-century visitors to the city that had become the vast capital of British India saw no memorial at all. Mark Twain, visiting Calcutta in the 1850s, records in his wonderful book *Following the Equator* that in the 'City of Palaces' – which already by that date had a population of more than a million people – he was put out not to see anything that commemorated a legend that was still so powerful that, he wrote, 'the mention of Calcutta infallibly brings up the Black Hole. And so, when [a traveller] finds himself in the capital of India he goes first of all to see the Black Hole of Calcutta – and is disappointed.'

Curzon – a great builder, and a great memorializer – therefore determined to present the world with a grander and more durable version of Holwell's original. It was erected on the same site as the first obelisk – at the north-west corner of what is now BBD Bagh, the original town square of Calcutta, with the original 'tank', or deep pond, of water to serve the townspeople, which still exists today. It was not the site of the Black Hole itself, but the place where the bodies of those who had died were thrown into a ditch for burial. We know what happened to the few, named, British survivors: the rest presumably just disappeared off back to their families or to whatever shelter they could find. The victims were buried unceremoniously and – because of the climate – as quickly as possible, piled together into a ditch by the nawab's soldiers and roughly covered with earth. There was no attempt at identification, no record kept, and – in a city famous for its elaborate and beautiful cemeteries – no headstones or markers.

As a more respectful way of marking this grim mass burial-place, Curzon not only copied Holwell's design – it appears prominently in every early print and painting of Calcutta – but inscribed the names of the dead on the octagonal sides of the plinth that holds the obelisk – or at least those names that he could find. Yet Curzon made some odd choices. He seems to have believed half the Carey story, for instance: Peter Carey's name appears among those who perished, but there is no Mary. Instead there is another woman's name, an Eleanor Weston, who is not mentioned in a single one of the early reports.

The evidence for Mrs Weston came from Mary herself, who surprised her journalist interviewer in 1799 by con-firming all Holwell described but 'added that, besides her husband, her mother, Mrs Eleanor Weston (her name by second marriage), and her sister, aged about ten years, had also perished therein'. Suddenly, another woman and a child are added to the roll. What's more, according to Mary, 'other women, the wives of soldiers, and children, had shared a like fate there'.

Yet if Curzon had taken Mrs Weston's name from Mary's report, why is Mary herself – who was by Curzon's day firmly part of the legend – not recorded among his carefully researched monument inscriptions?

One possible interpretation of this muddle is that Eleanor Weston was not Mary's mother but the person who later became her mother-in-law, since she married Captain Weston after she was widowed. But that does not explain why none of the other sources mentions Mrs Weston.

Amid all this confusion, Holwell, in his first letter and its postscript, says one of the few things that has the ring of truth about it, the kind that strikes a true note across the centuries out of the babble of distant voices: he says he doesn't really know. At first he names seven of the survivors, eight counting himself, and the rest were 'soldiers, black or white', whose identities he did not know. This is realistic – he would not have known everyone. Holwell was not Calcutta's military commander; that was Captain Minchin, who had deserted the fort and fled on a boat going downriver to the Dutch settlement at Fulta, along with Calcutta's governor, Roger Drake, and a number of other senior figures. It is a story of shabby behaviour.

So Fort William was defended to the last against tens of thousands of Siraj-ud-daulah's army by only a few hundred men, many of them native militia, whom Holwell would only previously have seen as part of a massed rank. Some were Portuguese and Dutch mercenaries fighting with the British, some – such as Peter Carey – were seamen hastily conscripted from the ships that happened to be in the harbour when the attack came. There were even some renegade French officers involved in the campaign (as there also were on the nawab's forces – there are reports that a special elephant

9

was deployed in the nawab's vast train at the Frenchmen's request to carry their wine, which is another example of the sort of story, almost certainly apocryphal, that gained currency at the time). Holwell also had no way of knowing whether some of the bodies found crushed on to the floor of the tiny room when the door was opened at dawn the next day might not yet have been corpses, merely unconscious: he was in no state himself to make a tally of the dead or of the survivors.

Over the centuries since the incident, historians within India and outside it have questioned and requestioned the official British version of events as launched by Holwell and enshrined by many others, including Lord Curzon. Holwell's own reliability was always in doubt, and during the long investigations that followed there was a sniping war of claim and counter-claim, allegation and innuendo and protestations of good faith. It was his general character and his self-interested motives that came under fire: Robert Clive, a letter-writer of unusual brevity and power, wrote home to the grandees of the East India Company that Holwell was a very able man, 'but from what I have heard and observed myself I cannot be persuaded he will ever make use of his abilities for the good of the Company'. In other words, he was lining his own pockets before all else. The battle over Holwell's veracity took place through pamphlets published on the streets of London, some of them long and complicated: one that runs to several pages, for instance, is entitled: 'A Vindication of Mr Holwell's character from the Aspersions thrown out in an Anonymous Pamphlet' and put out on 6 March 1764 'by his friends'. It was soon followed by others, wordily reworking old allegations, some of them very petty.

One way or another, it seems that at this time everyone sensed that there was something a bit fishy about the story and its most important witness. Nevertheless, as time passed and the protagonists died or ceased to seem important, it was the Holwell version of events that won the day. Most if not all nineteenth-century British commentators believed these basic facts of what Macaulay in 1843 called 'that great crime, memorable for its singular atrocity': this kind of language – 'crime', 'atrocity' – became the norm. Not only did the legend become that of a tragedy, but of a great barbarity. There were no 'aspersions' now, and the suffering British in the Black Hole were enshrined in the national record as heroic and innocent victims of a cruel power.

There was an alternative view among the ranks of the established historians, though, and especially towards the end of the century. It was not so much that the facts of the case were in question: it was more that a moralistic tone crept in. These apparently heroic victims of the Black Hole were not among the selfless ranks of the Indian Civil Service who later came out to administer India; these had been buccaneers, out for profit and individual self-enrichment. Not people who established courts and schools and railways but adventurers – entrepreneurs, if you want to put it politely in modern terms, or 'banditti', as they were sometimes less politely called in Britain at the time. They had brought with them most of their bad habits and few of their good ones, according to the upright and rather preachy H. E. Busteed in 1882, who called the Black Hole cell 'a vile and stupid importation of western barbarity' that 'went by the name that by an awful calamity has become historic'. Busteed seems to take the view both that the incident was a terrible tragedy and that it was the English traders' own fault. James Mill, in his enormous multi-volume *History of British India* as early as 1817, devotes a long, indignant footnote peppered with italics and exclamation marks to the hubristic nature of the place itself:

The atrocities of English imprisonment at home . . . too naturally reconciled Englishmen abroad to the use of dungeons; of *Black*

Holes. What had they to do with a *black hole?* Had no *black hole* existed (as none ought to exist anywhere, least of all in the sultry and unwholesome climate of Bengal), those who perished in the Black Hole of Calcutta would have experienced a different fate.

In other words, they built it and then they died in it and it was their own fault and it served them right. The trouble is, though, that both these apparently scrupulous and no doubt very well-meaning writers had themselves fallen into the myth-trap: in the face of plenty of proper evidence to the contrary, they obviously believed the Black Hole was a sinister dungeon, instead of an ordinary military cell of the sort that is common in any barracks anywhere. Whether the term existed before or not, it certainly passed into military slang. In the Hollywood movie *The Great Escape* the insubordinate prisoner Steve McQueen goes off to do his punishment time in 'the cooler' or 'the hole'; the Hole was the nickname given to an infamous windowless cell, number 14-D, in Alcatraz – since rumoured to be haunted.

Despite these disapproving voices, the story's iron-clad respectability throughout the Victorian era and into the next century can be gleaned from the historian J. H. Little, who wrote in 1915 in 'Bengal Past and Present' that 'it may be asserted with safety that every British schoolboy, almost as soon as he is able to understand stories at all, is told the story of the Black Hole of Calcutta . . . [and] . . . he never thinks of doubting the truth of the story'.

And why? Why should the nation have enshrined in its mythology this curious incident of the nawab in the night-time? Little is in no doubt that it was because '[the story] presents to the British nation a band of heroes not unworthy to rank with those who turned at bay in the retreat from Mons, with those who held the trenches at Ypres or those who stormed the bloodstained heights of Gallipoli'.

Since Little was writing while the First World War was still raging, there could hardly be higher or more emotive endorsement than this. Yet Little's purpose was not to praise this 'band of heroes' but to debunk them. He was 'amazed', he tells us after a long and wordy preliminary, in which he tries to establish his own disinterestedness, to visit Calcutta and 'to find highly educated Bengalis who disbelieve the story altogether'. And he goes on to explain why and how he came to believe the whole thing to have been 'a gigantic hoax'.

This was fighting talk. It was, after all, less than fifteen years since Curzon had elaborately remade the monument and the myth: a viceroy had taken time and trouble to research the records and inscribe in marble the apparent scores of victims, at his own expense; a respected historian reassessed the records and decided that nine people had been locked up in the Black Hole, of whom six had emerged the following day, the other three having died during the night of wounds they had sustained in the battle. This was Little's conclusion, and it is as plausible as any other – if we decide that Holwell and his few supporters were unreliable narrators with a vested interest in creating a dramatic and horrifying version of events.

So, in this bidding–war of numbers, the various historical accounts and explanations cover quite a range: nine versus 146 (the prisoners), three versus 132 (the dead). Recently, the British historian Linda Colley, in her book *Captives*, took a moderate course between the two extremes when she reckoned that the Black Hole probably contained about forty prisoners, of whom about eight died. Even Holwell's status as history-maker has remained contentious into recent years. Writers like Noel Barber, whose account of the incident written forty years ago stoutly defends Holwell and considers him to have been a hero, even if an unlikely one, pit their views against others such as Iris MacFarlane, writing in the

1970s, who accuse Holwell of deliberately lying and falsifying the record to further his own ends.

If a myth is a story that resonates because it tells us something more than itself, this is an unlikely candidate for mythical status. It wasn't really, in Macaulay's words, a crime or an atrocity: it was more of a mistake than a massacre, an ugly incident with tragic consequences for some, but hardly a bloodbath by the standards of eighteenth-century warfare. The translator of a contemporary Indian historian, Seer Mutak-hareen, points out in a note that in some versions of the loss of Calcutta it hardly figures: 'There is not a word here,' he says, 'of those English shut up in the Black Hole.' But in so far as it happened at all, the note continues,

The truth is, that the Hindoostanees wanting only to secure [the prisoners] for the night, as they were to be presented the next morning to the prince, shut them up in what they had heard was the prison of the fort, without having any idea of the capacity of the room . . .

These rather mundane facts, and others like them, could not be allowed to get in the way of a good story. The Black Hole's potential as a powerful fable, the kind around which nations cluster and define themselves, was spotted almost immediately. Perhaps it was precisely because of the lack of clear factual information that it was easy to weave a myth around the Black Hole: there was, after all, little solid evidence to get in the way, there were no pictures to establish a record, and because the old fort was so badly damaged during the siege of Calcutta the cell could not easily be visited later. It was eventually demolished altogether when a new fort was built in Calcutta – as Mark Twain noted, by the 1840s there was not even a site to be visited. It was also useful that the scene of the crime and its victims were half a world away from the scandalized London that received the news almost a whole year later: there was no one with whom to check information, no one to argue, and anyway by that time the Seven Years War with France was well under way, and other military scandals abroad, such as the loss of Menorca and the consequent trial of Admiral Byng, were keeping London's coffee-houses well supplied with weighty matters to discuss. 1756 was a bad year for the Byng family: while the Admiral was eventually court-martialled and shot for losing Menorca to the French (or, as Voltaire quipped, 'pour encourager les autres'), his nephew Robert Byng, still in his teens, was one of the youngest recorded victims of the Black Hole.

A good story needs a cast of characters, and Holwell supplied that in his personal account of 1757–8. It was written in the respectable literary form of a letter to a friend, but it was obviously intended for the public gaze (epistolary novels were in vogue at the time, and a formalized convention of letters was used for essays as well as memoirs and what we would now call travel writing). It was highly coloured – the historian S. C. Hill claimed that 'nothing more pathetic is to be found in the annals of the British in India'. Even so, it is not quite as highly coloured as Macaulay's description of it, almost 100 years later, when he thunders that 'Nothing in history or fiction, not even the story that Ugolino told in the sea of everlasting ice, after he had wiped his bloody lips on the scalp of his murderer, approaches the horrors which were recounted by the few survivors of that night.'

This was all good stuff, especially for the schoolboy market, and perhaps it was the narrative impulse that made Holwell feel he needed to put the spotlight on Mary Carey in his second version, when she had not even made an appearance in his first. There is simply no explanation for this – how, less than a month after the event, Holwell could have listed each survivor carefully, and somehow forgotten or failed to notice the pretty young woman among them. Others obviously felt the need for a beautiful young heroine too, and wove their stories with as little regard for the facts. The oddest thing about this historical puzzle, though – given that there must be countless historical events at which some characters sometimes appear, and at other times don't – is that Mary herself survived to tell her tale and to place herself within it.

Through the records of others, Mary appears and disappears like a phantom. Although one list puts her name among the European women who were dispatched on the ship to Fulta, another not only claims that Mary was not among them, but gives us a detailed and dramatic account of why not. The ship was the *Dodaldy*, and it was jointly owned by Lieutenant Manningham and Mr Frankland, two senior figures in Calcutta's hierarchy, who used the ship for the highly lucrative private trade in which everyone, from the military commander to the vicar, was engaged. (Information about ships, in this story, is much more reliable than information about people: in this kind of 'history', the ships almost become characters in their own right; more than that, their records were always meticulous, quotidian, precise. We may not know where Mary was, but we are in no doubt where the *Dodaldy* was.) As the few dozen European women and children were embarking, at night and in secret for fear of starting a panicked stampede among the thousands of Indian families huddled within the walls of the fort for safety – the native troops had refused to fight for the English unless their families were taken into the fort, and continued to bargain their safety in return for continuing to fight as the battle raged on – Manningham was overseeing the operation. No doubt he was anxious about the safety of his ship: such vessels were worth a small fortune, often the whole personal wealth of one of the Company traders, accrued over a lifetime. In fact, so keen was he to oversee the ladies' safe passage down the river that he felt it his duty to escort them personally, and then found himself too busy what with one thing and another ever to return to the besieged fort, where his colleagues were fighting for their lives, or to try to use his ship to rescue more of them.

Before the gallant Manningham ordered the *Dodaldy*'s captain to set sail, however, an ugly scene took place on the river bank below the walls of the fort. Mary Carey, this childless teenage wife of an ordinary seaman, had been working tirelessly alongside the grander European ladies, caring for the European children and for the sick and wounded throughout the siege. She was about to step on board herself – this is according to Noel Barber's 'lightly fictionalised' account – when Manningham rudely blocked her way, claiming that she could not embark: this evacuation was for European ladies, he claimed, and if the 'country-born' Mary went, what was to stop the soldiery demanding that all their many hundreds of wives should go too? Lady Russell, the senior lady of the small settlement, weighed in to argue for Mary; Mrs Drake, the wife of the governor, pleaded for her too, but Manningham was so firm that they had to bow to his decision, simply in order to get themselves and their children out of danger.

And that is supposed to have been the very unpleasant reason why Mary was the only woman left behind in the fort, to be captured the next night with the rest of the remaining English forces, and imprisoned in the Black Hole when the fort was forced to surrender. Did any of this happen? There are more inconsistencies. That there were several women and children among the Black Hole victims was recorded by Captain Mills, a survivor among Holwell's original eight, who writes of 'men, women and children' without estimating any numbers – but, oddly, infuriatingly, does not include Mary in his own list of survivors. John Cooke, another East India Company servant who left a record of the events of that night, specifically says there was only one woman, but does not name her; Holwell never mentions any children, even in the 1757–8 account, which was written for general publication. And since its palpable aim was maximum emotional effect, surely he would not have omitted piteous details of suffering and dying children.

In other words, when it comes to working out what exactly happened, who exactly was or wasn't there, who lived and who died, it probably cannot now be done. Holwell didn't know (but seems to have made it up), Curzon couldn't find out, and we shall never be sure. Historians can vary so widely in their accounts precisely because there are so few unarguable facts. It was an ugly incident, perhaps rather a pathetic one, but it was not a massacre – it was almost certainly a sad blunder. And, sorry as we are for the victims, it was not an exceptional death-toll. In the previous four days of fighting for the fort at Calcutta, as many as 5,000 Indian troops had lost their lives: but we do not know who they were. As with every other kind of history, it is the few known and named characters that shape the story, never the anonymous masses. Why these 132 (or perhaps three) victims became so important in Britain's island story was perhaps most succinctly expressed by an American. It was Mark Twain who called the incident 'the first brick, the Foundation Stone, upon which was reared a mighty Empire – the Indian Empire of Great Britain'.

It is a huge claim. He follows it with a useful canter through the events that followed:

It was the ghastly episode of the Black Hole that maddened the British and brought Clive, that young military marvel, raging up from Madras; it was the seed from which sprung Plassey; and it was that extraordinary battle, whose like had not been seen in the earth since Agincourt, that laid deep and strong the foundations of England's colossal Indian sovereignty.

Yes and no. It is certainly true that, in order to recapture Calcutta from the victorious Siraj-ud-daulah, Robert Clive sailed from Madras as soon as the news was received there with a fleet under the command of Admiral Watson, and at the battle of Plassey in February of 1757 he retook the city, dispatched Siraj to an ignominious end and established a sympathetic ruler, Mir Jaffir, on the throne of Bengal – but this by politicking and intrigue and deals done in advance rather than by a military feat to rival Agincourt. The idea that 'the British' – by which Twain probably meant the government – did this out of outrage about the Black Hole is of course not accurate, simply because news took so long to travel that Britain didn't even know about the loss of Calcutta until well after it had been regained. In fact, because of winds and tides, and the times of year at which the events took place, Calcutta's loss was known in London only a couple of weeks before the news arrived of its recapture, though the events were separated in real time by seven or eight months. What is more, the loss of Calcutta was not so much a disaster for national pride as for the national pocket; it was a financial catastrophe of huge proportions for the East India Company and its many investors. It affected the British government, and the nation too, because the taxes paid by the immensely profitable eastern trade formed a large part of the national exchequer – but it was still, for the time being, East India Company business. That it led to a revision of that view is undoubted, however: in that sense, Twain was quite right to have seen the loss of Calcutta as a turning point, not only a profound change in the avowed intentions of the East India Company but also a springboard for the imperial expansion that swiftly followed.

At the other end of the mighty nineteenth century, the ebb and flow of the national mood about empire – in Britain as well as in India – is neatly captured by the time-line of

Curzon's memorial. In 1902, the grand city of Calcutta was still the nation's capital (it was not moved to Delhi until 1911) and Builder Curzon was busily planning and creating even more mighty and beautiful things – the elegant Government House, for example, and the Victoria Memorial, a white palace that is still one of the city's treasures – while the great Bengali and Marwhari families who had grown rich from trade constructed their magnificent palaces too. Mark Twain waxes lyrical about the 'cloud-kissing' monument, a 'fluted candlestick' built by Sir David Ochterlony, one of the 'handful' of Englishmen, Twain says, who by

high achievements, duty straitly performed, and smirchless records . . . govern the Indian myriads with apparent ease, and without noticeable friction, through tact, training, and distinguished administrative ability, reinforced by just and liberal laws – and by keeping their word to the native whenever they give it.

In fact there was little that was selfless about Ochterlony's rather brash celebration of his own military campaign in Nepal. Even if Twain's was a rosy view, it reflects the climate in which Curzon raised his monument to the Black Hole victims at the bustling heart of the huge city. Yet, less than forty years later, the city's authorities decided they would have to move the monument – although traffic congestion was given as the feeble reason, the real cause was that it had become a rallying-point for Indian nationalists, especially the important nationalist leader Subhas Chandra Bose, and it was decided tactfully to put it elsewhere. Today it can be found in the farthest and most weed-filled corner of the churchyard of St John's church, which was built by the English in the late eighteenth century – surrounded by stray cats and litter, broken glass and bits of barbed wire. It is as unloved by Calcutta's citizens as it ever was – even if they are aware of it. Manish Chakraborti, an architectural historian and conservationist, considers it a poor 'piece of branding' for the city. Calcutta's reputation is still suffering, in his view, from the legend of the Black Hole.

2. In Search of the Nutmeg

The British Empire began to end in 1931, when the British parliament passed the statute of Westminster that gave equal dominion status to Canada, New Zealand, Ireland, Newfoundland, Australia and South Africa. Even then it was far from simple: in fact Canada had been a self-governing dominion since 1867, at which point some other parts of the Empire were still growing. Australian conservatives opposed the adoption of the statute until 1942, and Newfoundland never accepted it – Britain resumed direct rule in 1934 and continued until it became a province of Canada in 1949. At the other end of a lengthy process, it was not until 5 August 1962 that Jamaica celebrated her liberation from British rule, after more than 300 years – the island had been among the very first British possessions, in 1655 – and elected to join the Commonwealth. There have been very recent applicants, too: Cameroon, for instance, became a member of the Commonwealth in 1995, even though only a tiny part of her territory was ever under British dominion.

The ending of this mighty empire was typical of its existence: always multi-faceted, always contradictory, always a patchwork of differing needs and aims and aspirations. It always thrived on numbers, on scale, on impressive metaphors. The idea that the sun never set on the greatest empire the world had even seen was imprinted on to the consciousness of myriad schoolchildren, and it stayed there – a vibrant image that seemed somehow part of a geography lesson, an immutable physical fact like mountains or oceans rather than a statement about history or politics. Unlike other mighty empires, which met their end on a blood-drenched battle-field, or with a sad treaty, or fizzled out into bickering and apathy, the British Empire mutated into another astonishing parade of numbers and statistics: the Commonwealth of Nations, formerly but importantly now not called the British Commonwealth, to this day comprises 1.8 billion people in more than fifty nations among which there are thirty-two republics, sixteen constitutional monarchies and a handful of national monarchies – almost 30 per cent of the world's population and a quarter of its total land area. And these astronomical numbers are reached despite the fact that the world's best-known group of former British colonies, the United States, felt no need to join this entirely voluntary association, and more recently the former crown colony of Hong Kong returned to Chinese rule in 1997.

So that is how it ended. How it began was even more disparate, geographically, economically, sociologically and politically. The one thing, however, on which all historians seem to agree is that the British Empire began with stimulants. The cold northern people in their small draughty islands would, apparently, go to just about any lengths for a buzz. Over the course of its history both pre-imperial and imperial travel and trade brought us our mainstay comforters, sweet-eners and narcotics – tea and coffee, tobacco and opium, sugar, hempweed, spices and sweets and fiery peppers of all sorts – but it began, perhaps, with the apparently humble and domestic spices like cloves, pepper and nutmeg.

It's hard to imagine a world so dull and bland that it would be mad for nutmeg. If anyone these days has any association with this mild and sweetish spice, it's the scent of old-fashioned Christmases, mulled wine, an aunt's biscuits. It still occasionally appears in soufflés and cheese sauces, puddings and pies. In rather formal methods of cooking the French add it to béchamel sauce, Middle Easteners to mutton, the

23

Americans add it to all sorts of sausage, the Dutch and Scandinavians like it with vegetables. Pommes de terres gratinées dauphinoise cry out for it. Neither Burns' Night haggis nor Italian mortadella would be the same without that distinctive sharp-sweet aroma, so useful for disguising dubious meat; there is a sophisticated school of foodie thought that puts it together with garlic and mushrooms in northern Italian cooking, too. But it is hard to imagine it as dangerous, exotic, infinitely desirable and valuable, the substance of magicians and poets as well as traders, doctors and princes. Even more difficult to realize, today, is that one would kiss goodbye to one's loved ones and everything in the known world and take to a rickety ship, risking plague and pirates, life and limb, to sail to the edges of the map, to the tiny volcanic Banda islands of the Moluccas, in equatorial Eastern Indonesia, just to get this hard, dull brown nut.

Yet those tiny islands were a place of awe and legend, where the wonderfully named *Myristica fragrans*, mighty evergreens that rise 60 feet in the air, bear blossom supposed to have an aroma so heady that passing birds would be intoxicated and a fruit of succulent, tart white flesh, about the size of a small peach, that was celebrated by ancient Chinese and Indian savants under its Sanskrit name of jati-phala. The brown kernel of the fruit is the nutmeg itself, the surrounding red fibre is called mace – another and similar spice; both these, as well as the fruity flesh itself, are highly narcotic, even lethal in large quantities.

Measure for measure, nutmeg is vastly more potent than alcohol. All three parts of the fruit had an ancient reputation as a medicine, a stimulant, an aphrodisiac and a hallucinogen: not surprisingly, therefore, all the world loved it. Apparently, one could charge any price. Like all hallucinogens, it took on magical properties too, and was supposed to be lucky in gambling, in seduction, in politics and in perfume, for virility and against the plague; while the ground powder spiced up wine and food, the nuts themselves were used as amulets to protect against everything from boils to broken hearts. Then there were the 'nutmeg ladies' of the Restoration, when the spice gained a reputation as an abortifacient – which indeed it probably could have been, in sufficient quantities, since it is like all hallucinogens essentially a poison.

And – undated but potent in its political implications – there is the nursery rhyme 'I had a little nut tree / nothing would it bear / but a silver nutmeg / and a golden pear. / The king of Spain's daughter / would have married me / and all for the sake of / my little nut tree.' The silver nutmeg graters of the seventeenth and eighteenth centuries, with the finely worked little boxes that accompany them, hint at the full implications of the story: to merit such exquisite artifacts, this had to be a commodity of huge value and worthy of public show. Even up to Dickens' day, nutmeg-graters were personal items designed to be kept in the pocket. Among the paraphernalia of Georgian delectation – the asparagus tongs, the salts, sauceboats and wine coasters, the funnels and Stilton scoops and mustard pots – the nutmeg-grater is the one we hardly recognize today. But even into the early twentieth century, such *objets d'art* were made for the table, not for the kitchen.

By the ninth century, thanks to Arab traders, nutmeg and mace had reached the western shores: St Theodore the Studite allowed his monks to sprinkle nutmeg on to their pease pudding to sustain them on non-meat days, and Chaucer's libidinous Sir Thopas, when he is off in panting pursuit of the elf-queen he wishes to marry, did not forget his 'notemuge to putte in ale'. By the middle of the fourteenth century, a pound of nutmeg was worth seven fat oxen in northern Europe. A century later, however, the price dropped a little when the Europeans established direct trade links with

Indonesia – first the Portuguese with Vasco da Gama and Alfonso de Albuquerque, who made the earliest sprint in the spice race. They sailed east from the base they had already established in Goa, and by the early years of the sixteenth century completely dominated rival Arab traders in the Indian Ocean and beyond and set up a well-defended spice-route back to Europe for ships laden with nutmeg, mace and cloves, along with other valuable booty.

The British and the Dutch entered the spice wars, at the end of the century, when the secret of the source of these spices was discovered – the Portuguese had held their monopoly for many decades – and while some British commanders, notably Captain James Lancaster, who was soon to lead the very first voyage of the newly formed East India Company, found it easier to plunder returning Portuguese ships than to bother with trading himself, the Dutch sent a solid and well-financed fleet to the spice islands in the 1590s and relieved the Portuguese of their fort at Amboyna.

Now it was the Dutch who could operate a monopoly on spices from the east, and the nutmeg became the focus of a bitter international conflict between the Dutch and English – and earned its footnote in later economic history. The tiny Moluccan island of Run, where a tenuous British presence had been established at the start of the century, was held by a few men of the British East India Company against an onslaught from the Dutch until 1620, but after it was conceded the British eventually got their revenge on the Dutch through a treaty that ratified the Dutch possession of the spice island in return for the Dutch colony that included another, larger island – Manhattan. Some historians, when writing about the incident, fail to resist the quip about losing some small brown nuts but gaining a big apple.

The West Indian island of Grenada now calls itself the Nutmeg Island, its flag displaying the green, yellow and red colours of nutmeg and including a graphic image of a nutmeg in one corner. But that is because by the eighteenth century the nutmeg wars had become so fierce – the Dutch East India Company had established a vice-tight monopoly on the trade – that the desperate British and French had resorted to undercover methods. The French had smuggled seedlings out of the Banda islands and tried in vain to encourage them to flourish in another of their territories, the island of Mauritius, while the British did the same, with much more lasting success, on the island of Grenada. Every valuable and volatile market has its scams, too: in the USA, Connecticut was briefly dubbed 'the Nutmeg State' owing to a story that Yankee peddlers would sell whittled wooden 'nutmegs' for high prices to unsuspecting housewives.

What have nutmegs to do with our story, with Calcutta and with Bengal? This particular spice grew and flourished and was fought over half a world away, and since it was transported mostly by the Dutch ships it did not pass through the growing port at the mouth of the Hooghly river. But still the tale of the nutmeg has everything to do with Calcutta and its founding, its wars, its woes, its nature and its development. By thinking about the nutmeg we can begin to appreciate the lengths to which men would go, the distances they would travel, the dangers they would face and the uncertain outcomes against which they would pit themselves in order to – what? Sprinkle a little spice on their turnips? Pop a little powder into the wineglass of their lady love, hoping for a frisky night? To get away from back-breaking work on a wet dull farm in the Scottish Lowlands and fulfil a dream of exotic travel and even more exotic substances – literally to find, in the memorable phrase coined by the poet William Cowper in 1785, the 'spice of life'? Robert Louis Stevenson – a Scot, like so many of the early venturers – understood that the profits of overseas trade were only an incidental part of the urge to go in search of a fortune, of new lives and new lands. Empires were built on economics, and the profit motive was foremost, but that was obviously not an adequate way of explaining things. As Stevenson put it in 1878: 'We are told by men of science that all the venture of mariners on the sea . . . sprang from nothing more abstruse than the laws of supply and demand, and a certain natural instinct for cheap rations. To anyone thinking deeply this will seem a dull and pitiful explanation.'

What Stevenson understood was that if you wanted simply to play the laws of supply and demand, you might do better to stay at home and grow fatter sheep and bigger turnips rather than face immense risks on the high seas in search of novelties and luxuries. True, there were people driven to travel by economic necessity, especially the ordinary seamen on the ships that plied the oceans, and it is also true that the lure of possibly great fortunes was strong. But RLS understood that the urge to overseas trade was not really about what we needed, as a nation or as individuals, as much as about what we wanted, what we dreamed of: silks and diamonds, cloves and scents and all the perfumes of the Orient, new horizons.

But still, the first motive was to bring home a ship laden with a cargo that was light and portable and unperishable, yet one that sold for heavy, clinking gold. It was gold, and the dream of gold, that lay at the heart of most early exploration. The idea of enrichment came first; the notion of empire – which some have seen, crudely, as institutionalized plunder – came afterwards. The scope and longevity of the British Empire and its aftermath, which continues to this day with television news pictures of the Queen being greeted by distinguished men and women in feathered headdresses or saris or tribal scarification, gives the impression that the British somehow invented the imperial urge and were its first big players. Far from it. As the spice-race shows, the British were imitators, belatedly keen to get in on the act that the Spanish and the Portuguese had already mastered. By 1494, when the English were barely starting to think of economic expansionism, Pope Alexander VI had already issued a Bull that divided up the known world, allocating trade in the Americas to Spain, and trade in the East to Portugal. Trading with Asia, the Portuguese were growing rich on sugar and spice and all things nice, but the Spanish had their discoveries of precious metals in the New World.

And it was not as if the first European travellers were the first to sail any of those routes, or indeed to go in search of gold, spices or the other riches to be found far away. Nor – despite the appalling conditions and high mortality rate, as they blundered about the globe in ignorance of longitude and vitamin C – were they even unusually intrepid, by earlier standards. Herodotus wrote in the fifth century BC of the spoils of far-off lands, the gold, amber and tin as well as frankincense, myrrh, cassia and 'the gum called ledanon' (what we know as laudanum), as well as cinnamon that came from Africa (the ancients believed that the phoenix built its nest out of cinnamon), in a trade that involved journeys of 4,000 miles along the 'Cinnamon Route', from Indonesia across the Indian Ocean to Madagascar and up to Zanzibar, in outrigger canoes. Their sailors must have had a firmer grasp of geography than Herodotus himself, who believed that the world was symmetrical, with Greece at its centre, apart from his belief in flying snakes and gold-mining ants the size of dogs. And from India he hears of 'trees growing wild which produce a kind of wool better than sheep's wool in beauty and quality' – that is, cotton.

Other cultures were prodigious long-distance traders, too. Antony Wild, a historian of the East India Company, points out that 'whilst the much-vaunted Henry the Navigator of Portugal was still struggling to get his ships down the coast of north-west Africa', in the early fifteenth century, Chinese ships had long been in control of the Indian Ocean, and their spectacular seamanship allowed the grand Admiral Zheng He (apparently he was also known as the 'Three-Jewelled Eunuch') to parade at the court in Peking in 1414 a giraffe captured in East Africa and brought thousands of miles back on board an ocean-going junk. And the legendary Shah Abbas of Persia reversed the usual picture of east–west trade with a proactive approach, as modern business jargon would have it: he was offering to sell Persian silks to the western merchants while they were still trying to find their way to his country.

It is usually assumed that an empire means land. All these economically successful countries, however, and more like them, established their spheres of interest through travelling, and their skill in getting to a remote part of the world and home again with their cargo. Almost always, this meant journeys by sea. The earliest British 'empire', too – if we take an empire to mean an area of economic dominance – began to be constructed not on land but on the sea. The British searched for gold and silver in Virginia and elsewhere to no avail; meanwhile the Spanish had imported their slaves to haul the precious metals out of the mines of Mexico, Bolivia and Peru and – often with great difficulty, slithering painfully with their lame, silver-shod horses across the Andes – established routes down to the Atlantic ports, on to ships and off across the ocean back to a grateful kingdom. The prizes were huge, but it was all a lot of trouble: as with James Lancaster's later pragmatic approach to the obtaining of precious spices, other British seamen realized that there was an easier way to get at the gold they wanted. The vast, slow Spanish ships homeward bound from the eastern Atlantic ports laden with booty were a powerful temptation, especially for the smaller and nippier English ships that traded audacity and speed for might and firepower.

Piracy, some called it (especially the Spanish, and to this day in South America), but Elizabeth I decided that her 'privateers' were a superior class of robber, an entirely patriotic breed, and that the free-booting on the high seas in the late sixteenth century, with its enormous prizes of cash, silver and other commodities, was all a useful part of her campaign against the might of Spain. So although the prime motive was enrichment, this maritime activity was so political that some historians see it as a sort of undeclared war: Philip II was plotting to marry Mary Queen of Scots, overthrow Elizabeth and force Catholicism on England, and the sparring on the high seas was all part of a protracted test of strength between the two powerful nations.

All the great mariners of the time – Sir Walter Ralegh, Martin Frobisher, Sir Richard Greville and others – made voyages that were part exploration (always in 'greate hope of gold [and] silver'), part daylight robbery. The latter was often used to finance the former. Francis Drake's skill as a privateer was so much feared by the Spanish that their pronunciation of his surname (Drah-qué, which luckily means dragon in Spanish) became a byword for piracy on the high seas. He not only harried the great treasure fleets that sailed into the Spanish-held Carribean ports to pick up the gold and silver that had been brought laboriously overland from mines around the continent. In one famous expedition in 1572–3 he even went far inland in order to ambush one of the 'silver trains', the enormous mule-trains loaded with ore that made their painful way up from the south through the isthmus at Panama. The raid, which took many months in waiting and planning and fighting, was outright robbery, and there were not many such, but it was typical of much of what was to come, in one way: success came at a punishing price. The expedition caused scores of men to perish miserably of wounds and fever, several ships to be lost, and Drake himself to suffer the deaths of two of his own brothers – but he and the thirty survivors of the expedition returned to England very, very rich.

It set a pattern of expectations, perhaps: of very high risk and very high gain. For the whole of the next two and a quarter centuries, until the British Empire became administered by civil servants, and private profiteering was strictly forbidden, it was accepted that overseas trade and travel was a game of high stakes: life would be tough, and the expectancy of its duration pitifully short, but the fortunes to be made were as fabulous as the lands from which they would come. Almost until the dawning of the Victorian era there is hardly a single story of exploration and empire that does not include a death-rate that is close to that of the trenches in Flanders.

In a voyage of 1577–80 Drake became only the second man successfully to circumnavigate the world. The reconstruction of his flagship, first called the *Pelican* and then renamed the *Golden Hinde*, which now stands in a Thameside dock near Southwark cathedral in London, is astonishing however many times one sees it: it is so small. Making a full tour of the globe was of immense importance, at a time when British ships were trying to find a north-west passage, and had had little success in rivalling the superior navigational skills of the Portuguese that enabled them to round the tip of Africa.

The defeat of the Spanish Armada in 1588 sent a message that echoed around the known world. When, a few years later, Sultan Ala-uddin of Aceh, in Sumatra, graciously agreed to an audience with James Lancaster, himself a veteran of the Armada victory, the potentate's first words were of congratulation. The English ships had proved that the mighty galleons and carracks could be overcome, and that the overmastering Iberian command of the world's oceans was at an end.

Elizabethan self-confidence in the last decade of the century was high. England had become a secure and cultured place, an established power in Europe, and its self-awareness as a proud and successful Protestant renegade within Catholic Europe helped to define it as a prototypical nation state. Dreams of expansion, for an island nation, had to involve travel. Moreover, it had a rapidly growing population that was hungry for everything that commerce and overseas trade could bring them. Ambitious merchants were setting up a plethora of small companies – some had only one ship plying the seas in search of profit – trading with Virginia, Guiana, Moscovy, Persia; anywhere in which goods were to be had that would find a market at home. The usual method was a fairly simple one of a pool of investors getting together to finance a voyage or a series of voyages, splitting the profits if the ship came home, taking the losses if it did not. As early as 1555 there was the wonderfully named 'Mysterie and Companie of the Merchant Adventurers for the discoverie of Regions, Dominions, Islands and Places Unknown'; a merger of the Venice and Turkey Companies produced a 'Levant Company', and various bodies claimed the West African trade for themselves.

But investment was rapidly becoming more sophisticated, and the costs of launching successful voyages, especially to the spice-rich east, much higher. For quite a few years there had been a number of schemes designed to form investment alliances, but competition was always the stumbling-block. Everybody wanted to head east for a share of the market, but the various British ventures could hardly be racing against each other. It was bad enough to have to fight the Portuguese, whose monopoly in the spice islands still held, even if much more tenuously than before. Then there were the Dutch.

33

Already the most sophisticated capitalists of Europe, with a quasi-modern central banking and tax system and a system of public debt that allowed their government great financial flexibility, the Dutch were rapidly showing that well-funded voyages of trade and exploration had a much higher success rate. The English, their fellow Protestants in Europe, had suddenly become a more important competitor than their traditional Catholic enemies, and the English were also realizing the value of support from the state.

During 1599 and 1600, therefore, a group of London merchants was lobbying the monarch to provide a royal monopoly on trade in the east: it was, they argued, the only way in which their subscription of £30,000, raised to 'set forthe a voyage . . . to the Est Indies and other ilands and countries thereabouts', would be a tenable proposition. Only with such assurance, they claimed, could they provision and arm ships for the huge journeys to and from the east. After some persuasion, on 31 December 1600 Elizabeth I put her signature on the Royal Charter giving a fifteen-year monopoly over East Indian trade to 'The Governer and Company of Merchants of London trading into the East Indies' – usually known as the East India Company.

The 'First Voyage' of the new Company was in fact a small fleet – four ships, under the command of James Lancaster, which set off only two months later bound for Sumatra. Under the early system of the fledgling business, each 'voyage' was separately funded, and profits were at first extremely high. The investment was large, however: the initial £30,000 had to be supplemented with another, massive £30,000 in bullion, with which to pay for goods, as well as manufactured items for trading. Any losses were commensurately large – and with this first fleet the casualties began even by the time the ships reached the Cape of Good Hope. Captain Lancaster was considered very odd in insisting that his men each have a ration of lemon juice a day, and after the first weeks at sea the crew aboard his flagship, the *Dragon* (was this a sly reference to Drake?), were in good health, but the crews under the other three captains had become so weak that more than 100 died and the remainder had to spend time recuperating at Table Bay.

When they got to Aceh, in June 1602, to the sophisticated court of the sultan, then a great Islamic potentate, they found that the Dutch had beaten them to it. Not only had they got there first, but their resources were vastly greater. They could trump first the Portuguese, then the British, in terms of numbers of ships, manpower, provisions, and above all in buying power. That year, the Dutch too had set up their own East India Company, the Vereenigde Oostindische Compagnie, a permanent joint stock company that was far better capitalized than its London cousin. This first English expedition found itself stymied, despite the congratulatory welcome from the Sultan of Aceh, and Lancaster found himself resorting to a little light piracy, as well as trade wherever he could find it, to fill his ships' cargoes with pepper and spice. And although he had managed to establish a 'factory' – that is, a warehouse for the use of the Company's factors – in Java, he had been thwarted by the new Dutch stranglehold, and had established no lasting trade links with the area.

A footnote to this expedition underlines the sorts of risks involved in these lengthy early voyages. By the time Lancaster's ships got back to London, Elizabeth I was dead and James I was on the throne. The good captain had been away for three years, undergone extreme dangers, but his cargo was duly landed. However, James I himself had been investing in a little privateering of his own and his ships had just managed to capture two huge Portuguese carracks full of pepper. When Lancaster's pepper arrived to overload the market, the price dropped so severely that the Company's first proud investors had to take their profits in the form of quantities of small black peppercorn rather than the large clinking gold sovereigns of which they had dreamt.

3. The Making of Cities

The first steps in India were, for the English, the second-best option. Continually frustrated in the eastern spice islands, the fledgling East India Company started to look for trading opportunities nearer home, along the coast of the Arabian Sea to Surat on the north-west coast of India, in modern-day Gujerat. English envoys and traders were doing well in the Persian court and cities like Isfahan, with their rich pickings of silks, carpets, jewels and other luxury goods for the home market as well as for local trade and barter, so the bustling port of Hormuz was not only an important site for multinational trade in the area but also one in which English ships were becoming a familiar sight. With orders to see what could be done along that coast, the Company's Third Voyage set off in 1607, with spice-islands veterans in command – Captain William Keeling and the redoubtable William Hawkins, whose skill as a linguist, especially in Turkish, made him invaluable.

Again, though, the English were seen as unwelcome interlopers in the struggle for market share. Just as the Dutch were blocking the way in Sumatra, at Surat the Portuguese proved distinctly possessive of the trading arrangements they had already established: in fact their main aim, as Hawkins succinctly put it when he tried to anchor his ships outside the city, was 'to murther me'. He took an unusual decision: to leave his ships and goods under the best guard he could muster, hire a bodyguard of Pathans and guides and set off into the interior, on a journey of two or three months, to the Mughal court at Agra. There the Turkish-speaking emperor,

Jehangir, was sufficiently impressed by Hawkins and his ability to communicate that this unlikely first ambassador became something of a favourite.

Although Hawkins was far from being the first European to pay court to a Mughal potentate, he was unusual. At this date, the foreign traders – for all their power at sea – had only the smallest toeholds on the rim of the huge subcontinent, whose interior had its own evolved systems of government and commerce, its land routes for the conveyance of valuable commodities and its own sources of wealth. It is important to remember that when the Europeans first came to India (as with Persia and China), it was far from being a case of sophisticated and wealthy nations landing on the shores of a primitive country – as was the case in most parts of Africa. The wealth and culture of the Indian royal courts was fabled (even though the snooty Sir Thomas Roe, the next ambassador sent to Jehangir by James I, commented that he 'never thought a Prince so famed would live so meanly', he seemed to be alone in this view). The great mass of the people were not so different in east and west, at that time – historians who have done the sums reckon that in the seventeeth century, the Bengali peasant, for instance, had a way of life that was pretty much comparable to his counterpart in England or France, in terms of indicators such as nutrition and life expectancy. The growing European middle class had only a tiny counterpart in India, but in world terms the latter's trade, as historians such as Niall Ferguson have pointed out, was vastly greater in scale than England's at this date.

For all that Europeans had been plying their ships in and out of Indian ports for more than a century already – the Portuguese had set up an obelisk in Malindi, on the coast of East Africa, to commemorate the first successful expedition to land at Calicut, in the south, on the Malabar coast, as early as 1413 – they hadn't yet penetrated the interior of this mighty

38

land or had much to do with its population, other than the essential merchants and middlemen. Nor did most of them want to. Although the Portuguese fleet captained by Vasco da Gama in 1498 had arrived in Calicut with the expressed intention of shopping for 'souls and spices', the Protestant powers had no such missionary zeal. In Goa and elsewhere, the Portuguese made their Christian converts by a combination of pragmatic inducement and intense cruelty; the English, on the other hand, had little interest in making any at all. From the earliest days of the Company, traders had specific instructions not to interfere with local customs and religions, but rather to make common cause with them wherever possible.

This attitude continued, by and large: in later years, the administrators of the Raj did nothing to prevent missionaries from trying to convert Indians to Christianity, and, as the historian David Gilmour points out, there were evangelical Christians who 'decided that Hinduism was too benighted to reform – or even tolerate', and such figures as William Wilberforce, who 'believed that the conversion of India was still more important than the abolition of the slave trade'. But it was never part of any official policy, and, he says, 'the number of Christian converts was negligible'. The few official exceptions to the idea of non-interference, under British rule, were focused on specific cultural or religious customs rather than the religion itself, and these included the outlawing of the sati of widows and female infanticide. In an earlier time, if anything the East India Company's employees came to be remembered for their interest and enthusiasm for the eastern religions they encountered. William Dalrymple's portraits of eighteenth-century 'white moghuls' shows the degree of enthusiasm for Islam and its customs, or for Hinduism, among the foreign incomers to India, while in *Captives* Linda Colley quotes letters to show that as early as the seventeeth century there was official alarm about the way some captured ships' crews embraced the local religions and ways of life with such enthusiasm that they resisted their own rescue.

Leaving aside the souls of the population, from now on paying court to the Mughals became an important and time-consuming activity, involving vast and cumbersome baggage-trains of gifts, senior emissaries waiting around, sometimes for years, at the emperor's whim and one failure after another. For the moment, though, the British held on in Surat inter-mittently and by their fingertips, trying to extract from the emperor the all-important trading concessions and exchang-ing cannon-fire with the Portuguese galleons sent up from Goa against the English ships. Hawkins' high status at the Mughal court waned rather quickly, although not before Jehangir had provided him with a wife – though the poor woman arrived back in London a widow, since Hawkins himself had been a victim of the journey home.

Surat remained an important staging-post for journeys further east, and the Company did establish a large factory there, and despite continuing and savage warring with the Dutch, the Company's voyages eastwards in the first couple of decades of the 1600s were highly profitable and successful. But it was still a very long way round the tip of India and it was obvious that a base on the eastern seaboard would be an advantage.

That might have been, some would have said at the time, the only advantage of Madras, on the Coromandel coast of eastern India. It was an odd place for a maritime trading power to make a base, for the simple reason that it had no harbour, nowhere to land goods and no shelter for the anchored ships, which were perpetually in danger of being pounded to pieces – one later visitor called it 'the most incommodious place I ever saw'. The early accounts of land-ing at Madras are bizarre: the long, shallow tidal beaches meant that the ships had to anchor a long way out, and local boatmen with their dhurries and canoes would take off the passengers and cargo with painful and perilous slowness, then battle back to shore across the notorious 'bar', or sandbanks, and through the capricious rollers that usually left both people and goods deposited on land soaking wet, if not actually thrown into the water and having to swim for it. Nevertheless, Madras was welcome shelter for the British, who had again been cuckoos in Dutch or Portuguese nests up and down the Coromandel coast during the 1630s, facing hostility from their European counterparts as well as the warring court at Golconda, a local Hindu principality. In these years, too, a few factors were dispatched north to Bengal, already a thriving trading area up and down the treacherous Hooghly river, which despite its tricky tides and sandbanks formed one of the great waterways deep into the continent, and there they managed to get concessions from the Mughal governor of Orissa and establish a significant toehold.

It wasn't until 1639, however, that a Company man named Francis Day sailed down the Coromandel coast to the village called Madraspatnam, where he persuaded the local chief to grant him a small building plot, on which Day was determined to make a safe trading post for the British. It was a doubly odd choice: to the physical inadequacies of Madras (as it soon came to be called) was added the problem that it was only a few miles from the large Portuguese fortified settlement at San Thomé – almost in the enemy's camp, and certainly vulnerable. But if it seems peculiar, and unlikely, that what eventually became one of the most immense and powerful cities in Asia should have been founded more or less on a whim, by one man whose name we know, on a date that is recorded, then we have to look for small-scale and personal motives. These were not hard to find, and were well known at the time: Francis Day, it turned out, had a 'mistris' in San

Thomé and was so anxious to be near her that he staked his career on the unpromising new site at Madras, making extravagant promises to his employers about the much lower cost of cotton there and about defraying expenses from his own pocket, threatening to resign if his plans were not accepted.

The building of Madras' Fort St George, a basic four-square castle, caused much confusion on the ground, especially in relation to the local ruler, and much anguish to the Company's Court of Directors in London. But the £3,000 it cost turned out to have been a good investment: Fort St George still stands, mostly intact, with its adjacent warehouses, dwellings and church – it is nowadays the best way to see what these original 'factories', as the fortified offices-cum-warehouses-cum-residences of the new Company were called, looked like. Although travellers' tales of hair-raising landfalls continued, the unpromising new settlement was soon attracting weavers, merchants, shopkeepers and all the paraphernalia of a settled life and growing trade.

This was the first of the great three 'presidencies' established by the Company, and it was soon to be joined by Bombay and Calcutta, the places that later became the foundations of the Empire in India and three of the country's greatest cities. At first, these cities were 'effectively British-governed enclaves', as the historian P. J. Marshall puts it, but Calcutta and Madras were not British territory. Despite all the buildings and impressive possessions in their new settlements, the foreigners were leaseholders only, and their tenancy was at the pleasure of the local rulers. It was obviously an uneasy paradox from the start. This was 'expansion' – in Marshall's term – but not 'empire': that is, commerce, migration and the diffusion of British culture, but stopping short of imperial rule. Its inhabitants were what he called 'sojourners', who went out with the intention of returning to their homeland, not migrants of the kind that were going to the new territories in the Americas, or who went later to Canada, Australia and South Africa.

The presidencies each grew up in the same way as Madras, with a commercial imperative that brought not only the foreign factors and administrators but also the local merchants without whom they could do no business – some from the area round about, but often Marwaris from across the continent in modern-day Rajasthan (still renowned as some of the best businesspeople of the subcontinent), or Armenians from the Near East, Turks, Persians, Arabs and many others.

Each of these centres quickly became a racial melting-pot, certainly not the stereotype image of a small group of ruling whites lording it over a large number of local people. The new settlements were teeming with local labourers, certainly, but they quickly became a magnet for the Goan Portuguese who often served as mercenaries in the forces the Company soon assembled to protect its bases, Arab seamen who had put to shore, money-lenders from Constantinople, munshis (translators) and minor merchants, servants and a small army of people from around the world to service the needs of the incomers and to pursue their own dreams of greater affluence.

The next important and lasting Company base came about quite differently. When Charles II married the Portuguese princess Catherine of Braganza in May of 1662, the English Crown acquired its first real piece of land on the Indian continent – as opposed to the leasing arrangement by which Madras was built. It was only about 20 square miles of watery archipelago, most of it swamp and tidal waterways; it had a particularly filthy climate and it came with strings attached; but the Union flag could flutter there. It was the established Portuguese settlement originally called Bom Bahia (meaning 'beautiful bay', and indeed it does have that), and it was a dowry-gift to Charles II on his marriage to Catherine. Its existing buildings, some rather grand, should have made it an attractive proposition. But for the cash-strapped monarch it was nothing but an expensive nuisance. There was a clause in the dowry treaty that placed an obligation on the Crown to use Bombay as a base for defence of Portuguese interests in India, not only against the Marathas and other piratical local traders and rulers, but against the increasing might of the Dutch East India Company, the VOC – altogether an expensive burden.

So when in 1668 Charles leased the territory to the English East India Company, for £10 to be paid in gold, yearly, 'for ever', he was greatly relieved, and the Company inherited a strong base well placed for the lucrative trade with the Arabian ports. Bombay had the best of the harbours, and a good situation that allowed the building of country houses well outside the town. But its climate was so hard on the European constitution that it was the place where the infamous 'two-monsoon' rule was coined – with European life expectancy in the place averaging three years, it became axiomatic that only if a foreigner survived two monsoons had he a chance of living on; many didn't. And of English children born in the place, only about one in twenty survived their infancy.

Yet English children were born there, and lots of them. Almost accidentally, the Company had founded a colony. It had not wanted to: despite the general view that the East India Company was from the start an aspirant colonial power by another name – and as the direct forerunner of the Raj it can hardly seem otherwise – in these early years the opposite was the case. Despite their wish to defend their men and their goods, many of the Court of Directors in London were expressly opposed to acquiring territory, with all the expense of administration and civil responsibility that this entailed. From a purely business point of view, the rented factory at

Surat was perfect, even if sometimes unstable – it warehoused the goods, accommodated the men, served as a trading yard and stock exchange and even allowed such elegancies as were possible: roof gardens and a grand dining room, where case after case of drink could assuage the loneliness of the men – often very young men – posted there. But business isn't everything, especially when men are far from home for long periods, and have no idea whether they will ever get back there. In places like Surat almost the only women were the sort against which the chaplain fulminated; there was no sense of family and no sense of future. If there was disapproval about intermarriage with Indian women, there was almost more alarm at the many marriages with the Catholic daughters of the Portuguese and Goans.

So Bombay – despite the two-monsoon rule – was a magnet. The English left Surat in droves, attracted by the stability of ownership, and with them came the wealthy Parsee and Gujerati merchant communities, who soon contributed to the mushroom growth of the city. The Company quickly found that it had to adjust to the new realities unexpectedly foisted on them by their sovereign, and they had to change their rules to allow employees to stay on beyond their contracted term and settle if they wished. The Company actually decided to import women to its new territory – creatures who are spoken of in the voluminous Company correspondence exactly as if they were livestock. The governor would put in an order for supplies, the directors in London would endeavour to fulfil it, finding a cargo of 'civil' females, farmers' daughters and even 'gentlewomen' destined for the officer class. Not surprisingly, every woman declared herself a gentlewoman – and while many marriages and families ensued, the letters back to headquarters also report, slightly pompously and in euphemistic terms, considerable problems with 'impudence'. The conditions were harsh: no return tickets were issued. The women – or rather girls, most were very young – were expected to find a husband or some form of male protection within a few months: those that did not, presumably, just died. It was the first of what rudely became known as the 'fishing fleets' – women who went husband-hunting in the colonies – and although these early experiments were counted a failure, the fleets continued in various forms and became almost respectable by the nineteenth century,

The Company may have been playing God reluctantly, half-shocked at itself – 'our business is to advantage ourselves by *trade*,' the directors in London wrote to remind Bombay's governor, and perhaps themselves, in 1675 – but whether it liked it or not it was conducting a fascinating social experiment. And an oddly successful one. Despite the horrors of weather and disease, monsoon and shipwreck, within twenty years of Bombay's acquisition by the Company its population was as high as 60,000. Its early years were far from peaceful, with strife between the military and the merchant communities, but somehow within a handful of years there was an Anglican church, a string of fortifications, a mint, a hospital, a system of taxes and – most significantly, for the development of the other settlements – a judicial system. Now the men sent out purely to do business – men whose employers, half a world away, were warning them off civic expansion and administration, tartly writing: 'what government we have is [intended to be] but the better to carry on and support [trade]' – were raising taxes and dispensing justice, on Crown property. Half accidentally, the British throne had its first true colony in India.

Calcutta's story was a very different one. There's something about Calcutta. Even though it became a city with fine intellectual and cultural traditions, its founding was a grubby business. Of all the stories about Calcutta's first century of existence – roughly speaking, the eighteenth century – there are few that involve selflessness or heroism or even much decency. And there is hardly one about which all the sources agree.

The exception is a story about the man who is credited with founding Calcutta, a long-serving Company factor called Job Charnock. As the tale has it, in 1663, when he was chief of the factory at Patna, he witnessed one day a funeral pyre on which a beautiful young widow was about to meet an agonizing death in the flames, according to the sati tradition. Charnock was so smitten by her grace and her suffering that he snatched her from the pyre, married her, and he and the beautiful Maria lived lovingly together for the next twenty years, raising a family of four Anglo-Indian children. After she died he mourned her, peculiarly sacrificing a cockerel regularly on her elaborate grave.

That is the first and last nice thing anyone ever says about Job Charnock. He was a rough, cruel and autocratic character who was perpetually at loggerheads with his colleagues, and although long experience had given him a close understanding of local traders and merchants he was too brusque to get on well at Murshidabad or Dhaka, the chief cities of what was then the richest province of the Mughal empire, and where the local nawab, as the emperor's viceroy, held a sumptuous and civilized court. It was not surprising, according to one commentator, Sir William Hunter, that Charnock was 'not a beautiful person . . . for the founders of England's greatness in the East were not such as wear soft raiment and dwell in king's houses'. In a place where a man was old at forty, Charnock lived to an extraordinary age, well over sixty, which seemed to exempt him, at least in his own eyes, from some of the tenets of normal behaviour. And the town he founded, Calcutta – Kipling called it 'the city of dreadful night' – has few defenders. At the start, it was slightly too far upriver to allow proper access for the big ships, but too far downriver to be good for trading, and the goods still had to be relayed up and down by smaller boats. Captain Alexander Hamilton, who sailed in and out of the Hooghly many times, was alive to the danger of its shifting sands, whose perils were vividly illustrated by a huge broken-backed ship left on a sandbank as a warning. As elsewhere, the climate was awful: in his 'New Account of the East Indies' Hamilton fulminates against Charnock, who, he says,

could not have chosen a more unhealthful place in all the river; for three miles to the northeastward is a saltwater lake that overflows in September and October and then prodigious numbers of fish resort thither, but in November and December, when the Floods are dissipated, those fishes are left dry and with them putrefaction affects the air with thick stinking vapours which the Northeast winds bring with them to [Calcutta], that they cause a yearly Mortality.

To all the other hazards and diseases of Calcutta, then, had to be added the annual threat of dying from the smell of fish. Even more savage are the lines by Kipling in his 'Tale of Two Cities', when he describes Calcutta as a place 'Where the cholera, the cyclone, and the crow / Come and go', and recounts how Charnock:

> more's the pity!—
>   Grew a City.
> As the fungus sprouts chaotic from its bed,
>   So it spread—
> Chance-directed, chance-erected, laid and built
>   On the silt—
> Palace, byre, hovel—poverty and pride—
>   Side by side;
> And, above the packed and pestilential town,
>   Death looked down.

48

Nonetheless, this packed and pestilential town had been founded to order. If Madras came into existence for love of a pretty Portuguese lady, and Bombay through a useful dynastic marriage, Calcutta was the deliberate choice of Charnock, an old Company hand who was dispatched to find a base that offered certain advantages. The Hooghly river is a huge waterway that meanders down into a vast delta at the bay of Bengal, formed by the western branch of the Ganges together with myriad contributory rivers and streams that flow down from the mountains to the north and east. These days its waterway is highly controlled, but in the late seventeenth century it was a treacherous web of shifting sandbanks and tidal movement, but nevertheless navigable right up towards the northern parts of the province, and in another direction linked to the main stream of the Ganges. As a trade route, it was highly valuable. The Mughal city of Murshidabad presided over the best part; the rest was crowded with eager western merchants. The Portuguese had a trading post 25 miles upriver, until they behaved with too much arrogance for the liking of the local potentate and were dispatched; the Dutch were firmly settled by 1653 at Chinsurah (or Fort Gustavus), also well upstream; the French created a colony at Chandernagore (or Fort d'Orléans) in 1673 (this colonial possession outlasted even the British in India, as it was not handed back until 1951). Others, such as Danes and Venetians, are recorded as plying their vessels up and down, loading up where they could with cloth of all sorts, sugar, saltpetre and other valuables.

There is another sentimental story surrounding the first British concessions along the Hooghly, recorded a century later by Charles Stewart, among others. In 1636 Shah Jehan, the emperor who succeeded his father Jehangir, was still in mourning for his beloved wife, Mumtaz Mahal – for whom he built the Taj Mahal – when one of his daughters was badly burnt in an accident. Help was sought from one of the ships trading in the Deccan, whose surgeon, Mr Gabriel Boughton, successfully treated the princess. When asked by the grateful emperor to name his reward, Boughton selflessly asked for his country's right to trade freely in Bengal, and to establish factories at Ballapore and Hooghly, villages on the river bank, as well as at Kassimbazar, just 5 miles from Murshidabad.

That anecdote is typical of the self-congratulatory tone of some of the later commentators, as well as being, no doubt, a useful one to produce in justification. One of the most important local commodities, saltpetre, was enjoying a lively market at home by the 1640s, with the outbreak of the Civil War and the need for plenty of gunpowder, so the English factories on the Hooghly were especially important, and trade from 'the Bay' became as lucrative as that from 'the Coast'. During Cromwell's time, the demand for spices was as strong as ever (puritans were allowed spices, while other stimulants were prohibited); with the restoration of the monarchy the fashion for vast dresses of rich silks and brocades worn by both men and women refuelled the fabric trade and the demand for other luxuries.

However the royal agreement with the Mughal court came about, it was very valuable. Its terms were that the English could trade in Bengal exempt from the usual customs duty on their goods in return for payment of an annual lump sum to the ruler. By Charnock's day Shah Jehan had died and the throne had passed to his son Aurangzeb, an ambitious character who had ousted his father in old age and won out in the battle for succession among three brothers. The Company's annual subventions had to be renegotiated with every succession, and usually much more often than that – whenever his imperial majesty put pressure on the local nawab to come up with some more foreign silver and gold to finance his never-ending military excursions against the Afghans and the

Marathas. Yet since the English were well aware of this need for their imported coinage, they were in a strong negotiating position and could threaten to withdraw from any particular area – which would have spelt disaster for the new economies that had already come to depend on the trade in cotton and silks. 'All in all then,' the historian John Keay puts it, 'an uneasy and unwritten reciprocity underlay relations between the Company and the Moghul authorities. Instead of fleas on the back of Aurangzeb's imperial elephant, the European companies were more like egrets busily delousing the Moghul water-buffalo.'

This symbiotic relationship did not, however, prevent the outbreak of a miniature war with the Mughals in the late 1680s – a great stupidity on the part of all concerned. Every port was affected, and all along the Hooghly the foreign trading posts were being harried and attacked by the nawab's forces so severely that, after some fierce fighting, Charnock and all the rest of the Company personnel were forced to take refuge in Madras. At the same time the Company's base at Surat was becoming increasingly untenable, after many stormy years of trouble between the militia and the merchants, and the Company receipts were telling a grave tale of the financial consequences of losing the Bengal trade, in particular. The instructions from Leadenhall Street were clear and urgent: find a secure settlement in Bengal and fortify it. Aurangzeb called an end to the hostilities that had been raging around his kingdom – the Bombay garrison had finally had to submit to him – and restored trading rights. And the nawab of Bengal was not averse to the Company's return to the area, since his imperial master in Delhi was impatient for supplies of the foreigners' gold to be resumed.

So Charnock set out again, on the Company's orders, to find a site for this increasingly important trading post – and unwittingly inspired Kipling's gloomy lines of verse. As to when and how he chose this place for which no one had a good word to say, there are various options. The 'official' Company version of events has it that it was in 1690 – more exactly, on 24 August of that year, a date that is still commemorated in some quarters in Calcutta – that Charnock set himself up in Sutanati, one of three small villages not far from the mouth of the river delta, which were soon amalgamated into what became Calcutta (the name was an anglicized version of one of the three villages, called Kalikata). But as to how this came about, we can take our pick from a number of options.

One version has it that a benevolent and generous Aurangzeb granted the site to the Company in gratitude for provisions for his troops in the south, or (in a variant account) for Charnock's own help in subduing some unruly subjects.

Another, more highly coloured account claims that, after a ferocious skirmish gallantly fought by Charnock and his men, they were driven down the river to Sutanati and beyond, but the Mughal forces were in awe of their show of strength and made an advantageous peace treaty that included the lease of the lands that would become Calcutta.

A third possibility, and this was the reason favoured by some contemporary writers who thought the choice particularly obtuse, was that Charnock chose the site purely because it had a huge shady tree on the river bank under which he liked to sit and hold court.

But the most likely is, of course, the more complex, and has much less to do with the advent of Charnock. According to most modern Indian sources, Sutanati and its satellite villages were already a thriving if scattered trading community, and Charnock, far from creating the place, merely located himself within it. Long before Charnock, the area was a popular centre of the cult of Kali worship, and according to Nisith S. Ray this brought 'an influx of priestly class, the Tantric worshippers, the high-caste Brahmins and also professional classes incidental to and indispensable for a growing temple-town'. In addition, a network of forts had been built along the banks of the Hooghly after the Mughal conquest of Bengal a century or more earlier, and these outposts had been staffed by military and civil officials. The zamindars and merchants who moved inexorably in the wake of this quasi-military activity are well recorded, and some of the most substantial families, the Seths among them, seem to have been clearing the jungle and building trading centres, encouraging an influx of weavers and workers from neighbouring areas and organizing handloom weaving as a commercial venture well before the English arrived. So much for the Company version, which has Charnock arriving on a bleak shore peopled only by a few half-naked primitives scooping fish from the marshes.

Geoffrey Moorhouse mentions in his book on the city a curiosity that supports the notion that Calcutta already had a sophisticated population in pre-Charnock days. The anglocentric version of Calcutta's founding has it that Job Charnock issued an invitation to Armenian traders to come to 'his' new town, to take their time-honoured place in the running of things: their fame as shrewd and energetic businesspeople was well established. But in an Armenian churchyard in Calcutta, in the middle of a teeming bazaar, one of the piled-together grave slabs is a piece of black granite carved with an inscription to 'Rezabeebeh, wife of the late charitable Sookias', and dated 21 July 1630. Whether this is a 'slip of the mason's chisel', and that it should read 1730, or whether it is proof that the future capital of the Raj had actually been founded by Armenian merchants from Isfahan more than half a century earlier, is still a matter of debate.

Whether or not they were first, once the English did arrive in Calcutta, the quarrelsome spirit of the curmudgeonly old

Charnock, the 'man who loved everybody should be at difference', in the words of a contemporary, seemed to dominate the place. Everyone was at loggerheads with everyone, apparently. From London, the Company directors poured out a stream of letters full of complaint and criticism, railing at their hard-pressed employees for their weakness and timidity in not attacking and seizing another of the fortified sites in the area. In Bengal itself, the factors bickered and dithered, not helped by the fact that that Company had dispatched a ship – a year before, because that was the time the sailing took – with orders that completely contradicted more recent orders in letters. At home in England, political events in the last two years – at the end of 1688, the Catholic James II had been forced off his throne, to be succeeded by his Protestant son-in-law, William of Orange – had had huge repercussions for the Company, with a series of agreements and amalgamations between the English and the Dutch which had the advantage that the warring with the VOC would be at an end. But the 'new' Company was now sometimes at odds with the ranks of the old, leading to more quarrels and dissent on the Indian subcontinent. A combination of these upheavals, a new wave of successful interventions by the hated 'interlopers'– individual merchants who repeatedly tried to defy the Company's monopoly – and the recent wars against the Mughals meant that profits had taken an alarming dip. In 1691 the value of the Company's annual imports was a mere £80,000, for all this frenzied activity across half the world: seven years earlier, in 1684, they had been ten times that amount, at £800,000. Things were not going well.

In the new community at Calcutta, too, things proceeded very slowly. After a year, Charnock and his men were still living in tents and huts, 'in a wild, unsettled condition', with no factory or even elementary 'go-downs', as the storehouses were called. Alexander Hamilton describes Charnock sitting under his spreading tree, doing deals and dispensing rough and ready justice, but there were no proper building projects. The nawab, because of all the recent disputes more convinced than ever that the British were an uncouth and quarrelsome bunch who could never make up their minds (he much preferred dealing with the well-organized Dutch), had skittishly declined to grant his *parwanna*, permission for building works, and the coveted *farman* from the emperor himself was as elusive as ever.

In 1693, just three years into his new project, Job Charnock joined the numbers in the already swelling graveyard plot. The next agent in Bengal, Charles Eyre, played a very different part in the city's history. Whether or not Charnock was Calcutta's founder, Eyre was undoubtedly its architect. It was all in the family, in a way, as Eyre had married one of Charnock's Anglo-Indian daughters, and he was obviously a better diplomat than his irascible father-in-law. When a few years later a local rebellion in West Bengal caught the nawab unawares, and the whole west bank of the river was taken by the rebels, Eyre offered the services of the Calcutta militia to the nawab, and saw off the rebels for him. In return, he was granted the right to build what he needed to defend his own settlement.

4. Fortune Hunters

'Though our business is only trade and security, not conquest,' as the East India Company directors put it in one of their countless letters from London, 'yet we dare not trade boldly or leave great stocks where we had not the security of a fort.' So a fort was what Charles Eyre now determined to give them, as a first step towards the creation of a great trading city, and he had the tact to call it after the new king, Fort William.

The directors at home in London were aglow with pride. By 1699, never mind that the proposed fort was still in embryo, they were grandly announcing that:

Being now possessed of a strong ffortification and a large tract of land, hath inclined us to declare Bengall a Presidency, and we have constituted our Agent (Sir Chas. Eyre) to be our President there and Governor of our ffort, etc, which we call ffort William.

In a stroke, the fledgling city was elevated to a presidency to stand beside Madras and Bombay, with Eyre as its leader. However, the idea was still some decades short of the reality. As Busteed tells us, 'So cautiously and gradually was the fort constructed, that it took nearly twenty years before it could be called a fortification.' Since there was no stone of any kind in the swampy countryside around Calcutta, it had to be built of 'pukka' brick – the building material that gave an eloquent term to Indian English. But although 'pukka' (which originally meant 'baked') came to mean solid, correct and reliable – as in a pukka sahib, a proper gentleman – the original pukka brick was a sort of fiction. It could be made to look like stone, and appeared massively strong, but in fact pukka turns friable and crumbles quite fast in the Bengal climate. It is tempting to see it as a metaphor. Nonetheless, Fort William appeared to be an impressive construction, raised high above the river bank, commanding the water along one whole side of its substantial length. Its shape was an irregular rectangle enclosing a space about 210 yards by 120, with four towers at the corners and long curtain walls with parapets on each of which eight or ten cannon, ordered by Eyre from Madras, were mounted.

The directors, fortunately for us, arranged a detailed (though perhaps slightly idealized) representation of their newest settlement. In 1730, the East India Company decided to record on canvas some striking images of its international might, paintings to hang on the walls of its enormous revamped offices in Leadenhall Street, in the City of London. While the Company was building enthusiastically around the world, its premises at home were expanding too: its original half-timbered Elizabethan building had been modestly topped with a wooden carving of a cheerful sailor between two equally smiling dolphins, reflecting its simpler aspirations as a sea-going trader, but by this time the Company had come to occupy a great Georgian building that ran half the length of its City street and boasted a huge boardroom with a specially commissioned suite of wide and ornate mahogany armchairs, upholstered in claret-coloured velvet so thickly and stiffly embossed with the Company's coat of arms embroidered in gold and silver thread that they must have been thoroughly uncomfortable to sit on. Some of these can now be seen on display in the British Library in London; the first thing that strikes one is their remarkable size. These look like chairs made for giants, more like thrones than ordinary seats, and this no doubt reflected the directors' sense of self-importance

– a sense that was not entirely exaggerated, given the extraordinary nature of this commercial organization that founded cities and recruited armies, fought wars and moved whole populations, and brought back to England a substantial part of its national wealth.

Above the august heads of these grandees of commerce, in their Court of Directors, a fine lozenge-shaped ceiling painting displayed a neo-classical scene of 'The East offering her Riches to Britannia'. It shows a lightly draped and peachy-skinned female perched high on a rock, goddess-like, attended by a large sour-faced lion and a lounging Neptune – the nation's might by land and sea – and a full-rigged sailing ship in the background. She delicately picks a string of large pearls from the overflowing platter of jewels being humbly proffered to her by a kneeling, dark-skinned woman, behind whom is a queue of various indistinctly native figures clutching a porcelain vase, bales of cotton, all the images of wealth, trade and plenty, all ready to be poured into the lap of Britannia as if it were her elaborate birthday party. (This painting can now be seen in the Foreign Office in London: it is probably a very bad influence on those who walk under it every day.) It is not a bad painting, in fact – cool blues and browns in a flowing composition, and a dash of military scarlet draping the white-skinned male figure directing operations. He is dressed as Mercury, but he is clearly Mars: the armed power that oversees this apparently peaceable scene. Despite its superficial serenity, though, the picture purveys a message that is not only crude (and, to most modern eyes, offensive) but highly inaccurate. The image of a prostrate East simply handing over her goods, even if under a hint of duress, hardly reflected the complicated political realities and the subtle balance of power that had to be sustained both financially and diplomatically in pre-imperial India. It is no wonder that so many of the men who sailed eastwards armed only with the profit motive in one hand and this ludicrously crude notion of how the world worked in the other should have proved to be thoroughly deficient diplomats and negotiators.

Sitting on their thrones, under such a ceiling, the directors surrounded themselves with images of the places they themselves had never seen, but which were the source of all this might and wealth, pictures of the Company's settlements and factories around the world. The grand painting of Calcutta commissioned in 1730 from the landscape artists George Lambert and Samuel Scott shows the newly completed Fort William as massive, imposing, impregnable. It was perhaps also a sort of fiction. Spacious and hefty as the building certainly was, its pukka walls were only 4 feet thick and 18 feet high, above the level of the lower floor of warehouses.

It hardly mattered: thanks to one special diplomatic coup, the British position seemed unassailable. Some years earlier, in 1717, Calcutta's president, Robert Hedges, had declared a grand celebration – 'next Wednesday we make a public dinner for all the Company's servants and a loud noise with our Cannon and conclude the day with bonfires and other demonstrations of joy'. The reason for the 'joy' was that after a mission to the emperor in Delhi that had lasted several years, after a plethora of attempts, endless waiting and many tons of official gifts hauled across the country on long baggage-trains, a conscientious factor named John Surman had at last obtained the imperial *farman*. This was like the crock of gold at the end of the rainbow. It bestowed permission to trade freely, confirming all the Britishers' previous rights and privileges and adding more, with 'possession of several lands in many parts of India with such favour as has never before been granted to any European nation' – John Keay describes it as 'the Magna Carta of the Company in India'.

There were lavish celebrations in each of the British settlements, particularly in Madras, where ceremonies involved parading the *farman* to each corner of the town, bonfires and cannonades and 'feasting of the soldiers with tubs of punch'. Such public display, as Keay points out, was only partly an expression of genuine delight at a piece of paper which represented the keys to the treasure-trove, for the Company but also for individuals; it was also a way of making it clear to the local nawabs that the British held a trump card in the balance of power, the favour of the great emperor himself.

By the early 1750s, Calcutta had become such a busy and prosperous place, growing with extraordinary speed, that its European inhabitants seemed almost dazzled by the rapidity with which they could make money and reinvent themselves and their lives. The fort, despite the name, was more devoted to offices, residences and storage than to military activity. It was a town-within-a-town, the humming heart of the settlement. At ground level, with access straight out to the riverside 'ghats', was a honeycomb of warehouses, sited for the convenient loading and unloading of the boats on the river. Above this basement of storehouses was the main deck of the fort, consisting of a huge parade ground in front of the governor's grand residence, which was nearly 250 feet in length and towered above the level of the surrounding walls. At the other end was Writer's Row, a building that housed the young Company recruits in their meagre cell-like rooms, all the offices of Company business and everything else that was required for the bustling life of the place, a dispensary, storage areas for weaponry, food and military necessities, a vault in which valuables were stored, and so on.

Along one long side, bordering the huge parade ground, there was an arcade of open stone arches, which gave shade and protection from the weather. One small section of this arcade had been walled in to make the military lock-up, the Black Hole. Over the years, as trade relentlessly grew, the underground warehouses had not proved big enough, and more 'go-downs' had been built up against one side of the fort, all along its south side: to make access easier, holes had been knocked through the main wall into these flimsy structures. On the south side, too, it had seemed easier just to knock a few holes in the defensive walls, so that carts and labourers could more easily come and go to and from the lower warehouses.

Under the enthusiastic design of Charles Eyre, the town started to have a shape. Immediately to the south of the fort was dug the Great Tank, a huge pond or small reservoir that still exists today, at the centre of BBD Bagh, modern Calcutta's central square. It provided the people with water and made a focus for cool evening walks in The Park, a bare rectangle of several acres next to the tank from which the jungle had been cleared and where a few flowering trees and shrubs had been planted in hope. Just outside the walls of the fort on the land side was built St Anne's church, and a little further away the inevitable graveyards; elsewhere there were a Portuguese church and an Armenian church, as well as a 'pagoda' and of course countless temples and mosques in the rapidly growing labyrinth that was known, for obvious reasons, as 'Black Town'. In this space, by the mid-1750s, about 200,000 people were already crowded into a jumble of roughly built dwellings, selling food and vegetables brought in from the surrounding countryside, working at their trades, providing the labour for everything the fledgling city needed – an extraordinary number of people for a settlement that had been established only seventy years before.

The area around the fort where the Europeans lived – 'White Town' – was an elegant contrast to the teeming alleys of Black Town. As well as its park, its church and its playhouse it boasted a courthouse and a gaol built along The Avenue, a single straight road running up to the east gate of the fort, impressive for the time, wide enough for two carriages to pass. And, quickly, a ring of ever more imposing mansions, which over the years leading up to 1756 got larger and grander, stretched hundreds of yards along the banks of the Hooghly. Pukka brick could be made to emulate all the furbelows of grand Georgian architecture and create huge houses of dozens of rooms, complete with their gardens and stables and compounds of servants' quarters and kitchens, to satisfy the competitive aspirations of these newly rich traders. It was common for these houses to be of three storeys, of which the top one was something like a loggia, more or less just a roofed space left open to catch the slightest breeze to alleviate the punishing summer heat – there was no glass in any of the windows anyway, since it was not made locally and could not be transported. At the windows instead were slatted blinds made of thin linen, which would filter the beating sun and could create a moment of coolness in the hottest weather when the servants would douse them with water.

Mark Twain provides a fascinating detail about the realities of life in such a house, at least by the 1840s, when he visited the town. He tells us the summer heat in Calcutta was so searing that it could melt brass, and so the ornate brass doorhandles which were de rigueur at that date could only be used in winter, to be changed in summer for porcelain ones. He was there in brass-handle season, the 'cold weather' – although, as he points out, 'When a person is accustomed to 138 in the shade, his ideas about cold weather are not valuable.' It was a phrase, he decided, that had come into use 'through the necessity of having some way to distinguish between weather which will melt a brass door-knob and weather which will only make it mushy'.

This skittish riff tells us a lot about the appalling weather conditions of the place, but, even allowing from some change in style and fashion by Twain's time, it tells us even more about the pretensions of a fragile community perched on the edge of an unknown continent a year's journey from home. Why did the occupants of Calcutta's new mansions bother with brass door-handles? Why did they not adapt sufficiently to use the beautifully carved and crafted wooden ones that would have been available?

The residents of White Town lived in a sort of bubble. Dressed in their stiff eighteenth-century European fashions – frilled silk shirts and brocade waistcoats, heavy coats, tricorn hats and sweltering knee-breeches for the men; the women in layers of silk or cotton, low and tight on the bust, laced in hard at the waist, hopefully made according to the styles eagerly gleaned from whatever information reached them on the latest ship that had put in to port – they emulated the elegances of life at home with all they could afford in the way of carriages or palanquins, servants and horses, furniture and fine wines. The few images that survive from this time – for instance the so-called 'Company paintings', which were commissioned from local artists who knew how to please and flatter the European eye – show everyone well dressed and correct, elegant and upright. Pukka, in fact. The men occasionally wore loose and cool Indian clothes, but it was obviously unusual enough to be noted, even in the records of meetings. Otherwise, the façade was maintained.

But it was a tenuous existence, not only because death always hovered close. With so many single European men, most of them very young, and so few women and families – by the mid-1750s, there were only about seventy women and forty children in Calcutta's white community – it was inevitably a peculiar environment. They had no choice but to turn inwards on themselves, in this curious hot-house of over-excited trading and under-achieved personal lives. Such a young community, with such a rapid turnover of inhabitants, mean that there were few family or other links: it was a conglomeration of strangers. There was little to celebrate, although parties and balls and picnics were organized, as well as the inevitable card parties and drinking parties for the bachelors. One of the few relics of their lives that has lasted down the centuries is their elaborate preoccupation with death and burial.

There is almost nothing left of mid-eighteenth-century Calcutta today: so much was destroyed in the siege of 1756. St Anne's church, where Peter and Mary Carey were married, was blasted to pieces in the fighting, and it was not until 1787 that St John's, a beautiful classical church modelled on Gibbs' St Martin-in-the-Fields in London, was built in the plot that had been the early town's main British cemetery, not far to the south of the old fort. It still stands, near BBD Bagh and the Tank, and the mughalesque domed tomb of Job Charnock is there in its graveyard. But even such a small community soon needed more room for the perpetual burials, and the 'Great' Cemetery, now known as South Park Street Cemetery, was established in 1767. It was at that time well outside the city, among marshy fields and patches of jungle and bamboo forest where Warren Hastings hunted tigers; now it is an oasis in the teeming modern city. Some of the tombs and mausoleums were moved to the new plot, and over the course of just a few years an extensive and elaborate necropolis grew up, with streets and alleys and avenues of great marble monuments shaded by flowering shrubs and towering palms.

It is an extraordinary place: there are cupolas and obelisks and pyramids and classical statuary, lavishly carved ornamentation and long, chiselled orations. These are so detailed that many provide a biography in miniature. The tomb of the 26-year-old Captain Cook, for instance, a high stone column, records how he died from his wounds after an epic sea battle against the French in the mouth of the Hooghly, during which he managed to overcome a French frigate, *La Forte*, release the English sailors held prisoner on board and return to Calcutta with the captured hulk as booty. Here we can see the grave of Charlotte Barry, the adored young wife of William Hickey, the celebrated memoirist who came to Calcutta in March of 1783. Charlotte did not even last the year: on Christmas Day she died, a few weeks short of her twenty-first birthday. There is the grave of 'Hindu Stuart', Major-General Sir Charles Stuart, a tomb originally surmounted by carved Hindu deities in deference to his adoption of that religion. Or Sir John Hadley D'Oyly, an English baronet who went to Calcutta at the age of sixteen and some time later married a young widow called Diana Coates. Although he lived to a good age, he finally succumbed to a 'nervous complaint', 'due to an inordinate use of the hookah'.

There are celebrated men here: Sir William Jones, founder of the Royal Asiatic Society of Bengal, a fine linguist who was reputed to have mastered dozens of languages, including five or six oriental languages, but never his own (he was a Welshman); Lieutenant-Colonel Robert Kyd, a distinguished botanist and founder of the East India Company's fine botanical gardens; judges and surveyors, soldiers and administrators. Achievements are honoured: the inscriptions detail brave military actions and even scholarship: one Captain Thomas Roebuck is described on his tombstone as 'examiner in Hindostanee, Bruj Bhasha, Persian and the Arabic language'. There are literary figures with a wider resonance, too: Lucia Palk, to whom Kipling wrote the sketch 'Concerning Lucia' in *City of Dreadful Nights*, and Richard Becher, the grandfather of William Makepeace Thackeray. Thackeray's parents were married in St John's church, and he himself was born in Calcutta and sent 'home' to school alone at the age of only five. His portrait in *Vanity Fair* of Josh Smedley, the rich, coarse and lonely 'nabob' from Bengal, is coloured by experience. Perhaps the most famous literary occupant of the cemetery is Rose Alymer, a nineteen-year-old who was sent out to live with her aunt, Lady Russell, perhaps as part of the fishing fleet, perhaps to remove her from the attentions of the writer Walter Savage Landor, whom she had met in Wales on holiday the previous summer. Within a year of arriving in Calcutta, Rose died of cholera, and her curious twisty obelisk, richly carved and about 20 feet high, has a typically sentimental and almost meaningless piece of verse that seems mainly to be a reproach to the 'inclement clime' of the place:

> What was her fate? Long, long before her hour
> Death called her tender soul by break of bliss,
> From the first blossoms to the buds of joy,
> Those few our noxious fate unblasted leaves
> In this inclement clime of human life.

Meanwhile, her name became much more famous back in England, when the distressed Landor published his own lines, to the admiration of his literary contemporaries:

> Ah what avails the sceptred race,
>   Ah what the form divine?
> What every virtue, every grace?
>   Rose Aylmer, all were thine.
> Rose Aylmer, whom these wakeful eyes
>   May weep, but never see,
> A night of memories and of sighs
>   I consecrate to thee.

Amateur poets are plentiful here, but the thing that characterizes most of the inscriptions is their extravagance. When a young policeman called Samuel Munckley Duntze died at the age of twenty-five, after only a few months in the town,

66

one wonders who knew him well enough to have chiselled into his tomb, at great expense, a record of his 'urbanity of manners and benevolence of heart, which made him beloved and admired by all classes and the pride of every circle'. Or who composed the long panegyric to Charles Weston (an Anglo-Indian who acted as secretary to Holwell and may have been the second husband of Mary Carey) that ends its paean of praise with a stern address to the living; 'Reader! This stone is no flatterer! Go and do thou likewise!'

Most of these people lived in Calcutta after the period of our focus, but their memorials give us the best account of the realities of life in the middle of the eighteenth century. Petty accidents and perpetual disease caused such fatalities. So many women died in childbirth, barely out of their teens. One family buried four babies within six years, none of them older than fourteen months. When someone did live a reasonably long life by modern standards, it was almost always with tragedy close by: Ann Chambers died in 1782 aged sixty-nine, but buried with her are two of her infant grandchildren, already orphaned. And the size and magnificence of the memorials tell their own story: where else would one find a 22-foot marble pyramid erected to the memory of a baby of a few months? The yearning for places far away is conveyed by the habit of putting the full place of birth, as well as the date: in this swampy jungle plot still stalked by tigers were inscribed the memories of Canonsleigh in Devonshire, Kelso in Roxburgh, Badgemore in Oxfordshire and dozens of others. But perhaps the single most eloquent fact is the habit of measuring life not just in years, or years and months, but in days. One little boy was buried at the age of '4 yeares and twentie days'. His name has blurred with his stone's erosion, but we can still read quite clearly that he was, according to his grieving parents, 'an Uncommon promising Genius'.

The reasons for all this funerary pomp are obvious enough.

The memorials are massive and permanent, confident and invincible, as if a rebuke to the dangerous and uncertain times in which their occupants lived. And, as the Calcutta historian Harold Holloway put it, the inscriptions' 'obvious exaggerations of worth' may have been 'due in part, and perhaps often unconsciously, to a desire to bring credit to their own small community located in a foreign land'.

Despite the closeness of death, in Calcutta the families and the lone men alike persevered in trying to make a life, in this alien place they had created. The vast residence within the fort was home to Roger Drake, who had become governor more or less solely because he had not died: by the Company's strict rule-book, the most senior trader became Calcutta's civil administrator as well. It was a system that contained the most obvious drawbacks. Drake seemed quite unsuited to the administration of a burgeoning town, with the complicated civic responsibilities of running a police force, recruiting and maintaining a militia, dispensing justice and punishment. Such men ran the place, but they had no qualifications and no experience for doing so; most of them had no interest in doing so either. Drake was both pompous and ineffectual, middle-aged at thirty-four, and had caused scandal within the little community because after his first wife died he had married her sister. (To marry one's sister-in-law was not at the time illegal, but it became so later, in the Victorian era in Britain: for some peculiar reason controversy raged around the Deceased Wife's Sister Act of 1835, which even became the subject of contemporary proselytizing novels, and provoked a joke in Gilbert and Sullivan's *Iolanthe*, until the Act was repealed in 1907.) Something about marrying one's 'affine', as the Bible had it in its list of incestuous prohibitions, made people uneasy, but such marriages were extremely common, especially in a time of very high mortality. Most were cheerfully tolerated, or scarcely noticed: the fact that the second Mrs Drake was more or less ostracized in Calcutta says more about her own dismal character and her husband's talent for making enemies than about the sensibilities of the place.

Among the 'ordinary' families, if there was such a thing, were Calcutta's notary, William Dumbleton, who lived along Rope Walk with his wife and two young children; not far away, the assistant chaplain Robert Mapletoft was coping with his sickly and unhappy wife Sarah, who was pregnant with their third child in the intolerable heat of the summer of 1756. Among the grander mansions south of The Park was one belonging to Captain George Minchin, commander of the garrison, who had almost nothing to do except to make sure that drunken sailors from visiting Indiamen and the Dutch mercenaries with whom they were usually fighting were chucked into the Black Hole to sleep it off. It was also Minchin's responsibility to make sure that Calcutta's defences were in good order, but he seemed to have thought there was little need to do so – despite repeated warnings. His adjutant, Captain Grant, lived almost next door; near by too was the other senior officer of the militia, Lieutenant Witherington, who was nominally in charge of artillery and supplies.

History can hardly muster a good word for either Minchin or Witherington, but it was the captain-commander who provoked the weightiest sarcasm. 'Touching the military capacity of our Commandant,' was one acerbic comment, 'I can only say that we are unhappy in his keeping it to himself . . .'

The author of this remark was John Zephaniah Holwell, the chief magistrate, a member of Council and, at forty-five, already a veteran of the place. His large and imposing house was right at the edge of the town, by the river, and although he was clearly very shrewd he was a man who always, somehow, seems to have been surrounded by suspicion and controversy. No one ever made specific accusations, and indeed Holwell was never impeached and brought to trial for financial misdealings, but the suspicions never evaporated. Robert Clive, in one of his pithiest remarks, said of Holwell's later promotion that he thought the magistrate 'unfit to preside where integrity as well as capacity is equally necessary' – though there were many who might have found this remark brought pots and kettles to mind. Holwell's private morals, too, were often in question, and he was accused of hypocritically psalm-singing on Sundays with his family while carrying on 'the closest union with another man's wife'.

We don't know nearly as much about Holwell as we would like to. So many of the people who travelled to India at this time were running away from something, wanted to change something or obliterate something, or were fuelled by such a passionate desire to alter the odds stacked against them by the social or financial circumstances into which they had been born that many altered their names or life-stories to suit the occasion. After all, few people who were socially or financially secure would have wanted to risk their lives in these dangerous places on the frontiers of commerce and empire. It is frustrating for the historian that there is often very little information (and a lot of people called Smith) and it sometimes gives a peculiar idea that these characters were heroes of a novel rather than real people caught in history's whirlwind.

Of John Zephaniah Holwell's background, though, we do know a little. His grandfather, also called John Holwell, was an eminent scholar and mathematician, a royal astronomer and surveyor of Crown lands. His son, another John, became a merchant in London, and succeeded to ownership of the family estate in Devon, but something caused this settled and prosperous family to fragment and flee – some have suggested it was their support for the Stuart cause. Whatever the reason, young John Zephaniah had the sort of peripatetic youth that turned him into a linguist and a traveller, and the financial circumstances that turned him into a risk-taker. He was born in Dublin in 1711. He went to school in Richmond, outside London, and then for some reason to a sort of mercantile college in Holland, where he learnt French and Dutch and bookkeeping. His father organized a clerkship in a shipping-house in Rotterdam, but the drudgery seems to have got the better of John Zephaniah and – though we have no idea why – he next appears in medical apprenticeship at Guy's Hospital in south London, where John Keats had trained only a few years earlier, under the instruction of an enlightened surgeon, Mr Andrew Cooper.

With a rudimentary knowledge of this ghastly trade – second surgeons were at that date little more than butchers and saw-bones, the men who held down the screaming patients in their agony or swabbed out the buckets full of blood – Holwell went off to see the world. He took a job as surgeon's mate on board an Indiaman bound for Calcutta in 1732, and one can imagine the gruesome scenes that would have been his everyday work, especially if there was fighting. But Holwell was, through it all, a student. Further voyages on various ships out of Bengal and around the area, as well as a prolonged stay at Jeddah, were an opportunity for him to learn Arabic, which he apparently mastered well. He signed on with the dangerous 'Patna Party', a fighting force of about 400 that would sally out annually from Calcutta to the factory at Patna, probably escorting bullion and other valuables. Finally, after a stint as surgeon at the factory in Dacca, he returned to Calcutta. 'In obedience to your commands of March 1742,' runs a dispatch from Bengal home to the Court of Directors, 'we appointed Mr John Zephaniah Holwell one of your surgeons in this establishment in the room of Dr W. Lindsay, who departed this life of a fever.'

At last, after so many years of wandering, Holwell was part of the Calcutta establishment: he was twice elected mayor, and after a visit back to England, which he had used to write a long critique for the directors of Calcutta's tax-collecting system (the Zemindar's Court), he was appointed 'perpetual zemindar' – a post that included duties as a magistrate – a 'covenanted civilian' with a seat in Council whose annual salary went skyrocketing upwards from 2,000 to 6,000 rupees when the success of his tax reforms became obvious. By the time of Siraj-ud-daulah's attack on Calcutta in 1756, Holwell had risen to be seventh in Council. He was already forty-five.

In a community of the size of Calcutta at that time, the attributes and the failings of the leading figures were likely to become exaggerated. Petty feuds were magnified; small transgressions loomed large. Calcutta in the mid-1750s was riven with jealousies and antipathies: the governor and the military commander, Drake and Minchin, loathed each other and never spoke; Minchin's adjutant tried to keep communications open with Drake, and therefore Minchin mistrusted him too. And so on.

There were a few very old hands, who had already lived in Calcutta for many years and seen such rivalries come and go. The Reverend Gervase Bellamy, for instance, who married Peter and Mary Carey in his church, St Ann's, was sixty-five years old in 1756, and had already spent thirty years in Calcutta – both these statistics were astonishing, under the two-monsoon rule. Fat, jolly, bibulous (he was reputed to have the finest cellar in the town), he too had made himself an extremely rich man through the legitimate private trading that was open to all, even men of the clergy.

At the other end of the scale there were dozens of very young men, who began as 'Writers' (clerks) in the Company's service in their teens, no doubt intensely lonely and bereft at first, living with the knowledge that they had a high chance of never seeing their homeland or families again, and an equally high chance of dying soon and painfully. Henry Lushington was one who had begun his Company apprenticeship in 1753 at fifteen, but he had survived the hard beginnings that all Writers endured and was making a success of it. He had thrown himself into the study of Persian and Indian languages, and by the time he was eighteen was a skilled translator of documents; he had learnt to augment his tiny salary – the Writers started on £5 a year – and laid the foundations of future fortune by trading profitable cargoes of raw silk.

Lushington and the hundreds like him were usually young men – little more than boys – with education and background but no money, who had come to make their fortunes if they could. The incentives were not only strong, but almost literally a matter of survival: the annual salary of £5 was about the same amount as a ship's carpenter on one of the Indiamen plying between Calcutta and London would earn in a month. And if a young Writer could not bear the climate and the homesickness and tried to get himself back to England, the captain of any of those ships would charge him about £100 for the one-way passage. The potential rewards were huge, though, and the history books are full of those who succeeded – just as Calcutta's ornate graveyards are full of those who didn't.

There were men like Elihu Yale, who rose to become governor of Madras; although he was involved in one of the perpetual financial scandals and was even dismissed from the Company for abusing his position, he held on to his Indian fortune, returned to London and used a part of his wealth to endow a small American college that became one of the finest universities in the Ivy League. It was named after him in gratitude. Yale had been born in Massachusetts, but his Welsh family moved back to London when he was a young boy. He spent twenty-seven years in India, where he had four children, three of whom survived. Yale himself was a survivor; he died in London at the age of seventy-two. He never revisited America; his grave in Wrexham records a travelling life: 'Born in America, in Europe bred, in Africa travelled, and in Asia wed.'

Now that it is increasingly common to scrutinize the origins of the wealth of great benefactors, Yale's activities in India have been called into question. But it is probably fruitless to try to investigate exactly how any of these merchants, whether they were Company servants or 'free' traders who acted independently, made their money. No doubt many of their trading practices would seem unacceptable to modern thinking. All of it depended on the use of very low-paid labour. There was no organized slavery in the Indian trade, but quite a number of successful merchants came to own ships that would have been involved with the Americas, and especially the sugar trade in the West Indies (the largest and most lucrative of all), and were therefore implicated in the African slave trade.

A close associate of Yale was Thomas Pitt, who founded a great political dynasty in England. The fortunes of so many British families were laid in this way that they are too numerous to list, and a large number of country mansions and estates were bought or built on profits of the eastern trade. The colourful Thomas Pitt is a character who shines out, not only because his grandson and great-grandson became prime ministers, or because one of the world's most famous diamonds was named after him. Although the name now sounds so respectable, Thomas Pitt was something of a rogue, one of the men who hovered around the fringes of the Company's activities, spending a lot more time on his account than theirs. In fact he had started out as one of the hated 'interlopers', a freelance trader in India and Persia and other parts of the East whom the Company had been so anxious to control that they had gone as far as persuading the nawab of Bengal to arrest Pitt, 'a desperate fellow of a haughty, huffing and daring temper' and 'one that we fear will not stick at doing any mischief that lies in his power'. But when the 'desperate fellow' decided to go legitimate, with the help of changes in the structure of the Company dictated by interests in Britain who perpetually challenged the monopoly, this unlikely example of poacher-turned-gamekeeper was a great success: Pitt became a fearless, resourceful and extremely able governor of Madras.

He had always been interested, for personal reasons, in how to transport back home the riches accrued in the eastern trade. In the absence of a banking system with international reach, there were various ways of doing this, mostly rather crude. Later on the records show the strange way in which the Company's employees became its bankers: the traders and officials would lend the cash-strapped Company large amounts in whatever part of the world they found themselves and reclaim it, sometimes many years later, with interest of course, when and if they returned to England. Pitt, however, had always been attracted by diamonds: the simplest, most portable, most valuable commodity. Until the later part of the eighteenth century, India was the only place in the world where diamonds were found, and the diamond mines at Golconda, in the Carnatic, had been the basis for a fabulously rich and sophisticated court for several centuries. The Dutch had been dominating the diamond trade for some time: India produced the stones but did not cut them, especially not in the 'brilliant' style which pleased western tastes, and such a large number of Indian diamonds passed through Amsterdam that it became, as it has remained, a world centre of the diamond trade and of lapidary skill.

Pitt had already sent back to Britain a number of diamonds, some of them for the Company, some for himself. He was accruing land and estates in England; he had already – in one of the landlocked interludes of his turbulent career as an independent trader – become a Member of Parliament. Then, after a few years in Madras, he began to negotiate with an Indian merchant called Jamchund for an enormous rough stone weighing more than 400 carats – about the size of a hen's egg. The stone had been sold to Jamchund by an English skipper who may have stolen it from a slave – or so the story went – who had found it in the Parteal mines and had managed to hide it in a deep wound in his leg, which he had made for the purpose. Some version of the story prompted the acerbic lines by the great satirist Alexander Pope:

> Asleep and naked as an Indian lay,
> An honest factor stole a gem away;
> He pledg'd it to the knight: the knight had wit,
> So kept the diamond, and the rogue was bit.

Pope originally ended the last line 'and was rich as Pitt', but even in those days there were libel laws. The implication that Pitt had stolen the stone reverberated for many years: he was forced to prove its honest acquisition to the Council at Madras, and much later an elaborate justification was published in the *Daily Post* in London.

Pitt sent the stone home with his son, Robert, in 1702. The cutting was done in London, and the diamond was reduced to 138 carats in the process – but even the 'cleavage' (the bits cut off) was valued at £7,000. The only trouble about this mighty jewel, however, was that it was too big and too expensive easily to find a buyer, and it took Pitt a long time finally to sell it to the Duc d'Orléans, the Regent of France, for £135,000 – a profit of about £110,000.

The world's great diamonds, like the Koh-i-noor, the blood-soaked Hope diamond and the Pitt, which was renamed the Regence diamond, have biographies of their own. Most begin in India with tales of theft and treachery that pinned legendary curses on them. The life-story of Pitt's diamond began in bloodshed, skullduggery and controversy, but it moved into the great events of history. In 1791, it was valued with the rest of the French Crown jewels, at about a million pounds of those days. During the Paris Terror it was stolen and buried in a ditch; one of the thieves, however, bargained its whereabouts for a pardon and sent his accomplices to the guillotine. It helped to put Napoleon on the throne of France: he pledged it to the Dutch government to raise sufficient funds to make a success of the Marengo campaign. When it was redeemed from the Dutch, it was placed in the pommel of the emperor's ceremonial sword, the centrepiece of France's Crown jewels, just as the Koh-i-noor is the highlight of Britain's. It can be seen today in the Galérie d'Apollon in the Louvre, sparkling innocently.

Although none of the skinny, nervous teenage boys sailing away from home in the service of the Company in the 1750s could have known the end of this story, every one of them would have known its beginning. They would have known the facts and figures, the legends and the exaggerations, and they would also have known that 'Diamond' Pitt had died peacefully at Swallowfield Park in Berkshire, one of his six country estates, at the age of seventy-three, a Member of Parliament, the father of a large and successful family, a respected man.

They would know of a hundred other success stories, too. It could be done. But to get started, they needed money and contacts, and guidance in this baffling new place, and these were provided by a variety of merchants and agents from around India and the Middle East, for whom Calcutta had also become a magnet. Their multiple roles made the commercial life of the place possible. They acted as middlemen, as interpreters, as fixers and enablers. Most foreigners in Bengal had a 'banian', a factotum who ran the household, kept personal accounts, acted as a business agent for a commission and may well have loaned his employer the wherewithal to engage in the business as well. Some of the Hindu merchants, like some of the Armenians, who became very rich themselves, acted as money-lenders to the young Europeans when they first arrived, and the older ones when they couldn't pay their gambling debts, or when a ship went down, or when an investment went badly wrong. By the 1750s, there were in Bengal some 'highly developed banking networks', according to the economic historian Sushil Chaudhury, especially those of the Seth family. Although eurocentric historians tend to give the impression that the main stream of trade was in the hands of the foreigners, with the Indians always as subsidiary agents, Chaudhury also claims that 'the proposition that European purchases were much greater than those of Asian merchants has been questioned'.

As well as their economic importance, the Asian merchants occupied an essential place in the political existence of the town, often as intermediaries with the local rulers. The most important such figure at this time was a larger-than-life Jain merchant named Omichand, the richest man in Calcutta and probably, given his involvement in everyone's affairs, the most powerful. He financed commercial ventures and took half the profits; he knew everyone's business and everyone's secrets; he acted as intermediary between the British and the nawab. Omichand was an immense mountain of flesh, so large that his gorgeous carriages and palanquins, as well as his flowing silk gowns, had to be specially made; he moved around the town attended by ranks of brilliantly liveried servants and guards with scimitars. His largest property was a lush garden and house on the outskirts of the town, but he also owned the grandest house on The Avenue. Omichand was the only Indian to live in White Town; Noel Barber in his book points out that that was 'a privilege that could hardly be denied him, since he had financed the building of the majority of the European houses'.

Other intermediaries were equally important in the on-going political game with the local rulers, and the names of Armenian merchants, in particular, turn up in the records of the time. It is a small indication of how complex and intimate were the relations between the various national and social groups. There was a hinterland between Black Town and White Town, and it was more varied than the stereotypes suggest. Here there were senior craftspeople – tailors and barbers and saddlemakers and carpenters. Here were sailors who had 'run' from their ships to try to find a settled life. Here was the point at which the different worlds met: according to Barber (he describes his account as 'lightly fictionalised'), Mary Carey lived at the meeting of Black Town and White Town, with her Indian mother, waiting for her English husband to come home from the sea.

It is difficult to get a precise picture of the Black Town of the 1750s, because it was burnt to the ground, and almost nothing survived. Much of it was likely to have been more or less a shanty-town such as anyone who knows India knows: a labyrinth of stalls and stores and workshops with every conceivable trade and object for sale, a jumble of piled spices, heaps of vegetables, tiny stalls, twisting lanes where chickens ran and pecked, and where people made their lives in imposs-ibly small spaces. But there were certainly areas that were built with more sophistication too. The Armenian church of St Nazareth, which still stands, was built in 1724, so it is more than half a century older than St John's. Today the Armenian community is small, but in the mid-eighteenth century it would have been a substantial part of the town.

Whatever their status, however, everyone in this town,

from the governor down to the most menial Black Town labourer, had come to Calcutta for the purpose of self-betterment, and none of them could do it without the others. Everything here was dedicated to one purpose: trade, and the making of money. Through the warehouses of the fort and the store rooms of Black Town passed calico and silk, tea, porcelain, diamonds, pepper, spices, jute and saltpetre for export, while the incoming ships brought the means to trade all this: lead, quicksilver, woollen cloth, hardware, above all gold bullion.

5. Middlemen

None of this could have happened without the ships. The East Indiamen that plied between Calcutta and London – as well as across the whole of the Company's trading empire – were far more than means of transport. They were a lifeline, and they had a life of their own. Their departures and arrivals were more important than the calendar – people did not say, for instance, 'I wrote to you on Tuesday'; instead they cited the ships' comings and goings. 'I have written to you already by the *Mercury* packet,' runs one letter home from Calcutta. 'This [letter] is in consequence of what advices are arrived by the *Harcourt*.'

It was as well not to rely on the calendar, because sailing times were wildly variable and seasonal. When Siraj-ud-daulah attacked Calcutta at the end of June, he probably knew perfectly well that it was the moment in the year when it was most difficult for the British to send for help, or to get it. From June to September the monsoon and the prevailing winds meant that progress by sea southwards to Madras and on round the Cape was almost impossible; in the winter months it was far easier. Depending on the time of year, voyages in each direction could take as little as five months and as much as twelve.

And for a variety of reasons, including storms and pirates and shipwrecks. When the East Indiamen put to sea fully laden (499 tons was the usual declared at the start, for the simple reason that Company regulations stated that ships of 500 tons or more had to carry a chaplain), they were often commanded by young men who were not even twenty-one years old. It is tempting to think that some of the voyages suffered a little from a lack of sea-going experience and skill in navigating. Years later, in 1804, the Company finally issued a rule that the ships' commanders must have 'attained the full age of twenty-five years', their first mates fully twenty-one. And when we think that even the children of rich families, such as the semi-royal but illegitimate Fitzclarences, the many sons of the future William IV and the actress Dora Jordan, were sent to sea at eleven or twelve, and at the time the city authorities in London had the right to send any orphan boy in their care to sea from the day of his tenth birthday, we get a bizarre image of these mighty ships sailing the world with their valuable cargoes commanded by teenagers and staffed by children.

But people grew up young, and by their early twenties many seamen had years of experience behind them. Young or not, they were important figures: when the captain of an Indiaman landed at any of the settlements he was given a thirteen-gun salute and the rank of a member of Council. At first the Company built its own ships, at East India Dock on the Thames, but it soon began the system of commissioning ships from owners who were also the principal investors in the voyage. This Maritime Service, as it was called, was not the same as the Bombay Marine, which was the navy of the Company based in India. The Bombay Marine was created to protect the Company's ships against pirates, not to carry goods and passengers, so these watchdog ships tended to be smaller, nippier and even more heavily armed. The Indiamen themselves were armed like warships, though, and their sailors knew that they would be lucky to get through a voyage without having to fight off plunderers and pirates and even British 'interlopers', hostile ships not only from the other European traders but from China, Persia, Arabia and elsewhere.

One of the best pictures of what the ships looked like at

this point is in the painting that Lambert and Scott produced of Bombay – the equivalent of the one they painted of Fort William and the Calcutta harbour. In the foreground are two Indiamen at anchor, each with three masts and a high back like a galleon. From the long bow-sprit at the front flies a Union Jack; at the back end, even more prominently, each ship flies the Company's flag, which looks very like a precursor of the Stars and Stripes, with thirteen horizontal bands of red and white, the upper right-hand corner squared off to contain a smaller Union Jack.

The Maritime Service saw itself as a corps d'élite, far superior to the Royal Navy. Conditions and pay were better, and there was the doubly lucrative business of transporting passengers, who paid high for their fares, and private money-making schemes. In fact the Royal Navy so coveted the crews that the Indiamen could attract, who were Americans, Portuguese, Dutch, Chinese and Lascars as well as British seamen, that they tended to help themselves. When the Royal Navy needed men, which it almost always did, their ships would simply wait in the Channel, order a returning Indiaman to stop and press-gang its able-bodied sailors. It is ironic to think that, after travelling the world, weathering storms and facing hostile peoples, fighting pirates and nearly dying of dysentery and scurvy, a seaman like Peter Carey could be within sight of the white cliffs of Dover and be forcibly 'pressed' into a completely different service, and probably forced to depart again without even touching shore.

We have a brilliantly detailed picture of life aboard the Indiamen from the *Memoirs* of William Hickey. He saw the press gangs at work on his first voyage, when twenty-two men were taken off the ship; a captain of the 24th Dragoons, on his homeward journey, also describes how, as the naval officers came alongside the Indiaman, 'every sailor writhed his limbs and features into the most ludicrous distortions:

some limped, some stopped, and all did their utmost to appear decrepit and unfit for service'. Even so, six of the most skilled seamen were taken away, and the Indiaman's captain was left to continue as best he could: sometimes the ships couldn't even move after the press gangs had paid a visit.

There were fights, even pitched battles, as men would do just about anything to escape the 'press'; the war of words at home between Leadenhall Street and the Admiralty was almost as bitter.

Despite all this, the Indiamen were an extraordinary opportunity for making money. There was a system of 'indulgences', by which the captain and other ranks were allowed so many tons of their privately owned goods carried back and forth – it was not only the ships' owners, and the Company, who were making large profits. This system was obviously open to a great deal of abuse, and there was always a torrent of official letters, orders and ever more obsessively detailed regulations about it. Later in the eighteenth century the 499-tonners gave way, despite the chaplain problem, to ever larger ships, and by the start of the nineteenth century there were dozens of juggernauts the size of battleships involved in the East India trade, 'a cross between a castle and a floating warehouse', which gave everyone more room for more cargo, more passengers, more profits.

As the ships became more and more profitable, everything was of course for sale – including the command. Captains paid the owners many thousands for the privilege, and the command of the ship was then the captain's property and could be transferred, sold or given away to a son. As well as the lucrative trading opportunities, captains pocketed the fares charged to passengers, which could be very steep. It is hard to think of a modern money-making scheme equivalent to these ships. There are recorded cases of a commander making as much as £30,000 on a 'double voyage' – that is, from

84

London to Bombay or Madras, then on to China and then back home – usually a round trip of about eighteen months. In modern terms, that would be about £1.5 million. But even if such sums were not common, in only a few voyages most of the commanders could expect to buy themselves a substantial property at home and retire to lives of leisure and ease.

On board ship, while the life of leisure was still a dream to be attained, the officers did very nicely for themselves. The captain had two servants, as well as his own cook and steward; other officers had similar sorts of privileges. They set up travelling homes on board, and decked out their accommodation as they wanted. William Hickey describes the cabin of a Captain Peter Douglas on board the *Plassey* in 1769 as 'painted of a light pea green, with gold beading; the bed and curtains of the richest madras chintz, one of most complete dressing-tables I ever saw, having every useful article in it: a beautiful bureau and book-case stored with the best books, and three neat mahogany chairs . . .'

For well-off passengers, life could be reasonably comfortable too. They were expected to furnish their own cabins, and this cabin furniture then usually furnished their homes when they got to their destination, or could be sold off on the quayside for (once again) a nice profit. Peter Cherry, a Company man in Calcutta, wrote to advise his daughters what they'd need to bring. On a 'regular Indiaman of not less than 800 tons . . . will be an abundance of room for your piano, harp, etc, hanging lamp and candles, 2 or 3 small bureaus with book shelves on them, 2 or 3 sea-couches with drawers to convert into sofas in the daytime, a wash-hand stand with two pewter guglets, foot tub and three chairs . . .'

And so on. These ladies were going to be a lot more comfortable than the poorer passengers, the Writers and young army officers. Ozias Humphry, a painter, travelled home in a cabin 9½ feet by 8½, but at least he had it to himself; the worst description comes from George Elers, a subaltern in the 12th Foot, who sailed to India in 1796 aboard the *Rockingham* in a cabin 12 feet square which he shared with ten others, four of them sleeping in slung hammocks and the other seven in 'standing cots'.

If that sounds the stuff of nightmares, it was still a great deal better than the conditions endured by the common sailors. Although the Maritime Service was supposed to be preferable to the Royal Navy, there were still floggings and other appalling punishments, endless back-breaking work and a terrible diet that decimated crews with disease even after the causes of scurvy were well enough known that the ships almost had whole farmyards on board. Peter Carey would have known what it was like to sleep 'literally upon one another and on the orlop deck the standing beds were three tiers high, besides those slinging'. These 'standing' beds or cots were exactly what they sound like: never mind the pianos and harps in the grand cabins, below decks the space was so limited that not everyone could lie down. To sleep in this kind of contraption you were strapped in to a sort of canvas bag that was tied to a wall or beam, which held you upright as you slept as best you could. And that was when you could sleep: seamen could be at their gruelling work for days and nights on end to keep the ship going. Between the disease, the dangers, the punishments, the battles with pirates and the exhaustion, it is not surprising that quite a number 'ran' – deserted – to try their luck in civilian life in one of the new settlements, well beyond the arm of the British law.

Yet even the ordinary sailors could have done a little trading, if they were clever. The shops in places like Calcutta were hungry for absolutely anything that could be brought from Europe, and it was through the private trading of the ships' crews that the new settlements could get the finer

things of life. Captains and officers liked to use their 'indul-
gence' or 'investment' on the outward journey for things like
saddlery, finely made boots, 'millinery and Madeira, claret
and cutlery, perfumes and glass-ware', as one account has it.
Charles Chisholm came to Calcutta on the *Gatton* in 1778
and brought with him a complete pack of fox-hounds, 'then
in great demand by Bengal sportsmen'.

The usual way of doing things was to sell the goods off by
advertisement. The *Calcutta Gazette* might tell the delighted
community that, for instance, Mrs Fay:

respectfully gives notice that Capt Roddam and Mr Burdekin's
investments of haberdashery are exposed for sale this day. Also a
complete assortment of Millinery from Madame Beauvois, which
has not yet been opened on account of the rains. N.B. In the above
are two very elegant suits of mourning.

Or that Mrs Creighton and Miss Tranter 'beg leave to
acquaint the ladies of the settlement' that they have bought
up all the millinery and haberdashery from one ship: 'most
superb suits of dresses of the latest fashion, a variety of most
fashionable dress and undress caps, hats, turbans, etc.'

Hickey records sales of jumbled assortments – everything
from confectionery to pickles, claret to cutlery, jewellery to
fishing tackle, even some of the food that would make exiles
yearn for home: cheeses, hams, tongues, Scotch barley. Such
was the way that these fledgling communities made their
lives, in some sort of imitation of what they aspired to at
home – if they ever got back there.

By the end of the eighteenth century, the sailing times
seem to have settled down into some degree of predictability,
and early in the year a ship that left London in January could
usually reckon to be in Calcutta by May. On the return, as
long as it was after September, about the same time would be

usual. But things went wrong, often. The very first trip to India made by Robert Clive, in 1743, would have been enough to discourage most people for good. The *Winchester* sailed from the Thames on 10 March. In the first ten days they got as far as Plymouth. On 18 April her consort ship, the *Princess Louisa*, went aground on one of the Cape Verde islands, and seventy of the crew were killed. They spent three days at São Thiago, another of the islands, and then sailed for the next twenty-four on the north-east trade wind. On 17 May the *Winchester* herself went aground, and they discovered they were on the coast of Brazil. The 'Treasure belonging to the Hon'ble Company' was landed, and there they stayed for four months, until a pilot arrived to guide them to a port where repairs could be made, taking another five months. When the *Winchester* at last weighed anchor in February it was to pick up a south-east trade wind to take them round the Cape of Good Hope, but a storm drove them into Table Bay; there they were forced to stay until April. Clive finally reached Madras in June – about 58 weeks after leaving London. The *Winchester* went on to Calcutta; three days after reaching port there, the commander, Captain Steward, died of fever.

Not only had it taken Clive so long to get to India, but he could not write to his father about his journey or his safe arrival until September, because of the winds.

Clive's long, slow story shows not only how perilous and unpredictable the journeys were, but also how erratic were the lines of contact. A letter could arrive from the Court of Directors in London issuing orders that had already long been countermanded, because a later ship had arrived first, addressed to a recipient who was dead or had himself long ago sailed away, about something that happened a year or more earlier. So although the Honourable Company ruled its far-flung possessions in what James Mill called 'an empire of copperplate' – reams and reams of perfectly handwritten letters and documents that streamed out of Leadenhall Street and on to the high seas – it was a tenuous management process. Everything was written down, in the closest detail – bills and accounts, receipts and lists and orders, instructions and rebukes and congratulations, hiring and firing and announcements of promotion – all the day-to-day business of a big, well-ordered company. But the way in which any of this reached its destination, and in which replies came back, was subject only to the chaotic laws of the wind and the sea.

So although the East India Company must have been among one of the most wordy and bureaucratic anywhere, one sometimes gets the impression that it was talking to itself for much of the time. Apart from the Court of Directors and Court of Proprietors, there were a plethora of committees, all passing paper backwards and forwards to each other, all requiring letters from the Company servants abroad. There was a Committee of Correspondence and a Committee of Lawsuits, a Committee of Treasury and one of Warehouses, a Committee of Accounts and a Committee of Buying, and a Committee of Shipping. There was a committee that regulated private trade, and another whose job was to prevent the growth of private trade. And so on. The Calcutta Council and other Company employees lived in fear of the directors' authority, because rules were strict and strictly applied, and huge amounts of time were spent replying to the endless badgering, hectoring letters from London. But in fact, a community like Calcutta ran itself, and its only real point of reference was Madras. It was too isolated for anything else to be possible. So when trouble came, all the power of the great Company meant nothing.

The effects of all this trading activity on the home market were of course immense. Expatriates languishing in Calcutta may have been overjoyed to get their Scotch barley and their pack of hounds, but at home the country had gone mad for foreign goods, the more luxurious the better. It wasn't only the rich who benefited, nor were they the only customers: social commentators of the time write about how Britain and its customs changed with great speed with the influx of previously unknown wonders from around the world.

By now the trade from 'the Bay' consisted of substances like saltpetre, spices, raw silk, nankeen cloth, drugs and perfumes (musk, camphor, arsenic), tea (it had been brought to India from China not long before, and the value of the trade in tea remained far greater than any other commodity). Another important berry had joined the nutmegs and peppers and cloves that had made up the first fruits of eastern trade. Coffee – 'the wine of Arabia' – had for some time been traded by the Company between the eastern countries, especially Persia, before it was known at all in Europe. Once it arrived in the west, though, it caused not just a revolution of taste but of social manners and customs, as the advent of the London coffee-houses provided an environment in which the rigid ancient class distinctions started to melt. These were places open to any man who was reasonably dressed and could pay for his 'dish [of coffee] and pipe [of tobacco]', whatever his background, and they even had an explicit egalitarian code – everyone who frequented them had to obey the posted 'Rules and Orders', which declared that all men were equal in these establishments, and none need give his place to a 'Finer' man. It is not surprising that the coffee-houses had quickly become the most important talking-shops, social meeting places and sources of news and gossip as well as literary and cultural innovation.

Apart from the fruit of camellia sinensis (tea) and that of coffea arabica (coffee), there was the fruit of the loom. The craze for Indian fabrics – silk and cotton chiefly, but also calicoes and muslins – is described by Niall Ferguson as 'nothing less than a national makeover'. It was captured by Daniel Defoe, that irascible man who was nonetheless a brilliant commentator on social mores. In 'Everybody's Business is Nobody's Business', a diatribe against the dishonesty and general uppitiness of the servant classes in England, he claimed that the influx of foreign luxury goods had raised aspirations and started to chip away at the social distinctions of dress that until recently had actually been enshrined in law. He even blames a degree of social chaos on Indian silks and satins, because they caused young men of good family to fall for 'the flirting airs of young prinked up strumpets' clad in the new fabrics. He fulminates that:

our servant-wenches are so puffed up with pride nowadays, that they never think they go fine enough: it is a hard matter to know the mistress from the maid by their dress; nay, very often the maid shall be much the finer of the two. Our woollen manufacture suffers much by this, for nothing but silks and satins will go down with our kitchen-wenches.

Moreover, the working classes' desire for imported goods meant that:

she must have a hoop too, as well as her mistress; and her poor scanty linsey-woolsey petticoat is changed into a good silk one, for four or five yards wide at the least . . . in short, plain country Joan is now turned into a fine London madam, can drink tea, take snuff, and carry herself as high as the best.

So it was not only the gorgeous fabrics that fired the import trade with an eager market, but these novelty stimulants – tea, coffee, snuff – 'of which the consumption in Great Britain is scarcely to be conceived of,' Defoe grumbles on, 'besides the consumption of cotton, indigo, rice, ginger, pimento or Jamaica chocolate, rum or molasses . . .' and claims that 'England consumes within itself more goods of foreign growth . . . than any other nation in the world'.

Back in India, it was a complicated process that supplied this appetite. Each different substance had its own method of growth or production, and all of them involved a long and complex chain of people involved in the business. One detailed description by James Mill – of the way the woven cloth trade was carried on – shows the intricate web of relationships on which both Indians and Europeans depended. And, being Mill, he spices his account with a strong moral perspective.

The weavers, like the other laborious classes of India, are in the lowest stage of poverty, being always reduced to the bare means of the most scanty subsistence. To transact . . . with each particular weaver . . . is a work of infinite detail, and gives employment to a multitude of agents.

He is not exaggerating about the 'multitude'. He goes on to explain a rigmarole that is almost Kafkaesque:

The European functionary, who, in each district, is the head of as much business as it is supposed that he can superintend, has first his banyan, or native secretary, through whom the whole of the business is conducted: the banyan hires a species of broker, called a gomashtah, at so much a month: the gomashtah repairs to the aurung, or manufacturing town, which is assigned as his station; and there fixes upon a habitation, which he calls his cutchery: he is provided with a sufficient number of peons, a sort of armed servants; and hircarahs, messengers or letter carriers, by his employer: these he immediately dispatches about the place, to summon to him the dallals, pycars and weavers: the dallals and pycars are two sets of brokers; of whom the pycars are the lowest, transacting the business of detail with the weavers; the dallals again transact with the lycars; the gomashtah transacts with the dallals, the banyan with the gomashtah, and the Company's European servant with the banyan.

This gives us an idea of what Henry Lushington and the other aspiring young traders had to cope with. This was the official part of their jobs, too: in order to take home that dreamt-of diamond, they would have also to get involved in this sort of protracted and labyrinthine negotiation for themselves. There were endless opportunities for cheating and being cheated, as 'the Company's servant is five removes from the workman; and it may easily be supposed that much collusion and trick, that much of fraud towards the Company, and much of oppression towards the weaver, is the consequence of the obscurity which so much complication implies'.

It was hardly surprising, given the number of people in this chain, each making a profit from the weaver's work, that the weavers themselves should be in terrible poverty. When it came to paying up, in this ruthless business, it worked like this:

Besides his banyan, there is attached to the European agent a mohurrer, or clerk, and a cash-keeper, with a sufficient allowance of peons and hircarahs. Along with the gomashtah is despatched in the first instance as much money as suffices for the first advance to the weaver, to purchase materials, and to afford him subsistence during part at least of the time in which he is engaged with the work. The cloth, when it is made, is collected in a warehouse . . . called a kattah. Each piece is marked with the weaver's name, and when it is convenient for the gomashtah, he *holds a kattah*, as the business is called, when each piece is examined, the price is fixed, and the money due on it paid to the weaver.

At the end of his recital of the process, Mill delivers his verdict:

This last [the kattah] is the stage at which chiefly the injustice to the workman is said to take place; as he is then obliged to content himself with fifteen or twenty, and often thirty or forty per cent, less than his work would fetch in the market.

So that is what happened at the lowest end of the production line. That piece of cloth woven by a poor Indian weaver passed through the hands of at least six or seven agents, then through the process of shipping, then through the selling and buying once it reached England, yet it was still affordable by the servant class and the 'prinked up strumpets' so hated by Defoe, and could turn plain country Joan into a fine London madam.

If this account shows us how deeply the European trade penetrated into the Indian population, and how whole industries and centres of employment would quickly build up around it, it also makes us wonder what the rulers of the place thought about such economic dominance by the outsiders. If they were so touchy about territory and building, what did they feel about the foreigners' control over so many people's economic lives? Mill is quite clear. 'This,' he says, 'is a species of traffic which could not exist but where the rulers of the country were favourable to the dealer; as every thing, however, which increased the productive powers of the labourers added directly in India to the income of the rulers, their protection was seldom denied.'

It is a resounding answer to the simple view of pre-colonial exploitation by the foreign powers: since the local rulers were themselves doing so well out of it, and so many local people getting richer too, with the possible exception of the poor weaver everyone was happy.

6. The Oppressors

Fort William looked so solid. Gazing complacently at the oil painting on the wall in Leadenhall Street, the directors could not have imagined that anything might be amiss. But they were a very long way away, and the two-monsoon rule was so implacable that it was not uncommon for them to receive information in London and immediately send a reply that only arrived some months after its intended recipient was already dead.

So it was that several of the Company's skilled engineers, who one after the other issued grave warnings about the true state of the fort, did not survive long enough to do much about it. Mr Boscawen had told the Bengal Council in 1748 that '[Fort William] does not appear to be a place capable of any prolonged resistance'; Mr Robins agreed, just before he joined his predecessor in the cemetery. By 1755, the place still seemed 'more like a deserted and ruined Moorish fort than any place in the possession of Europeans', according to a Captain Jaspar Jones of the Bengal artillery. By this he meant that the years of monsoons and excoriating sun had crumbled away the tops of the fort's walls and rotted the gun emplacements so that they could no longer support the weight of cannon. Those walls, too, had been weakened by the making of gateways and doorways that gave access to the warehouses. St Anne's church and many of the large three-storey houses of the Council members crowded so close around the fort that, even if a cannon had been fired, the ball would probably have gone straight into an upstairs drawing room. The next expert sent from England, Captain Caroline (sic) Scott, delivered his view that 1,000 European troops would be needed to defend the place 'as it is now fortified, *if we may be allowed the expression*'. As John Keay tells the story: 'Needless to say, both Scott and Jones submitted new proposals for rectifying the situation: both then died within the year, and so did Scott's successor.'

It is ironic, to say the least, that when trouble did come, it was on the pretext that the English had fortified their town too heavily.

In Calcutta in these years of growth and prosperity no one seemed worried. No one thought it worth investing in defence: Captain Grant, the adjutant, described the mood as 'so infatuate a security that every rupee spent in military service was esteemed so much loss to the Company'. There were always distant rumours of trouble and occasional skirmishes, and the threat of marauding Marathas and Afghans had even induced the nawab of Bengal, Alivardi Khan, to allow the British in 1742 to construct a huge ditch, or moat, to run in a wide loop all the way around the town, which already measured about three miles from end to end, enclosing it completely from the landward side and protecting it from attack. This was highly unusual: in his territory, Alivardi kept all the foreign companies on a tight rein, and they were never free to add to the fortifications of their towns and factories without the nawab's express permission. To do so would have been seen as an aggressive act, and invited the appropriate response. Alivardi used to reply sweetly but disingenuously to every such application, in a curious echo of what the Company directors themselves liked to think was realistic, by saying: 'You are merchants, what need have you of a fortress? Being under my protection, you have no enemies to fear.'

And when, as sometimes happened, the nawab's soldiers would surround one of the smaller factories upriver and blockade them for a day or two, it was almost a convention that what was required was nothing but a nice fat pay-off: the rulers well knew, as historians have remarked, that the longer their soldiers encircled the 'hatmen' the more they would pay to get rid of them. It was a sort of local taxation system.

Whether it was because of their looming fort, because of the paternal protection of a nawab who was more interested in solving disagreements with bags of gold than by the sword, or whether it was because they were simply too busy and happy making money and quarrelling with each other, the residents of Calcutta in the 1750s seemed to think themselves insulated from danger. To the south of the town the Maratha ditch was never finished – it was still swampy jungle just outside the town, where tigers and other big game could be hunted, and the construction of the fortification probably seemed like too much trouble. Along much of its length, too, it had silted up or been filled with rubbish: it hardly presented much challenge to an invasion force.

This neglect – and what one Calcutta resident described as the prevailing 'spirit of levity' – was to have grave consequences not only for the British and their employees, but for the local people too. As S. C. Hill put it in his study of Bengal published under the auspices of the government of India (i.e. the British government of India) in 1905, when the Raj was at its most confident and the tendency to be critical of the men 'in trade' who had served the East India Company at its most severe,

to the natives, who were unacquainted with the science of fortification, [the settlements] appeared strong and well able to defend themselves against any attack by the native Government. It can therefore be easily understood how there gradually grew up in the minds of the Bengali Hindus that if the worst came to the worst they might find in the presence of these foreigners a means of escape from the ills by which they were oppressed.

97

It might not have been only the natives who were 'un-acquainted with the science of fortification', but the British traders too, who were after all hardly qualified as architects or military strategists. That apart, Hill – with all the confidence of hindsight – is pointing to something that is probably less easy for us to see now, with the attitudes of a later age. The Bengalis, he says, at first saw in the 'hatmen' a possible refuge from their oppressors, rather than seeing them as being the oppressors. Bengal had already been governed for more than two centuries by oppressive outsiders, but they were Muslims, not Europeans. There was no love lost between the Hindu population and their Muslim rulers. British writers of the time were vividly aware of the situation: Colonel Scot wrote in a letter of 1754 that 'the Jentue [Hindu] rajahs and population are much disaffected to the Moor [Muslim] Government, and secretly wish for a change and an opportunity of throwing off their tyrannical yoke'. Since so much commerce was in the hands of the Hindu merchants, there was a natural alliance with the foreign traders, and it was a situation of which the nawabs were well aware. Close alliance between the Europeans and the powerful Hindus was a prospect the Muslim rulers most dreaded, one that had to be countered by every means.

From the western perspective, the history of India is a story about invasion and expansionism by European powers who subdued a native population. From another perspective, it looks rather different. Within the great landmass of India was an imperial power, relentlessly expansionist, that had imposed itself violently on the indigenous peoples, with its foreign religion and customs. But it was not the 'hatmen': it was the Mughals. During the early years of the European landings in India, the Mughal emperors, far from living in fear of incur-sion by these white-skinned outsiders, were busy expanding their own empire. The foreigners pecking at their coasts were an excellent source of revenue, and helped to fund their culture and their magnificent courts at home, as well as their military campaigns against their neighbours, but their armies were so huge and their command of territory so extensive that at first there was never much danger of losing out in the intermittent sabre-rattling that went on.

They had come from the north, from Afghanistan. Babur, the first Mughal emperor, seized power from the sultan of Delhi in 1526. He had an impeccable pedigree for an invader, since he was descended on his father's side from the Turkic Timur and on his mother's from the mighty Ghengis Khan (*mughal* comes from the Persian word for Mongol). These Muslims ruled over a country that was almost entirely Hindu, and over the next three centuries there was no dilution of their faith. They made many converts, however, over the years, and by the middle of the eighteenth century almost half the population of Bengal was Muslim, living mainly in the east of the province.

Because of the religious divide, too, the Mughals took care to surround themselves with armies who would not be likely to turn against them and side with the majority of the population, so they liked to employ foreign soldiers. They were skilful at holding a deft balance between the military, on which they depended for holding and expanding power, and the civil power of the great Hindu merchants, as well as the Hindu princes in other territories, such as Rajputana.

Akbar, the third Mughal emperor, was particularly adept at managing the religious question. He was reasonably liberal-minded as well as pragmatic and realized that it would be a good idea to win the loyalty of Hindus by appointing them to high military and political posts. At the same time he extended the system of nawabs − local rulers who acted as viceroys in the various provinces of the empire, who were often kinsmen and always Muslims. In theory the nawabs were appointed by the emperor, but in practice they often took the title by force and did their best to pass it on to their sons or nephews. As long as the new nawab pledged loyalty to the central power, and proved useful, the emperor was usually content. But the story of Bengal, in particular, shows how in this far-flung empire the minor thrones of the emperor's representatives were up for grabs, pretty much to all comers — as long as they were Muslims.

Babur made his capital in Agra, and it wasn't until his great-great-grandson Shah Jehan took the throne in 1628 that the centre of power moved back to Delhi. Under Jehan, who was a generous patron of the arts, the extraordinary feats of Mughal culture and architecture, a marvellous blending of north Indian, Turkish and Persian traditions, reached their finest peak. But when it came to the turn of his ruthless son Aurangzeb, everything began to change. He was a religious bigot who broke the delicate balance of power by trying to impose Islam on all his Indian territories; he harassed Hindus, dismissed them from public service and destroyed their temples. He spent the last half of his very long reign — it lasted almost fifty years — trying fruitlessly to conquer south India.

After that, the Mughal dynasty went rapidly downhill. Lord Macaulay described the bickering and lacklustre monarchs who followed Aurangzeb, none of them for very long, as 'a succession of nominal sovereigns, sunk in indolence and debauchery, [who] sauntered away life in secluded palaces, chewing bang, fondling concubines, and listening to buffoons'. The Mughals' main enemies — especially the dreaded Marathas — got rapidly stronger, and this confused power-vacuum made it easier for other outsiders to encroach. The last Mughal, a very nominal emperor, was ousted by the British in 1858.

Caught between their Muslim rulers and their imported mercenaries, the up-country Hindus wielding economic power and the other outsiders who played a significant role in the province – Armenians especially – the people of Bengal themselves were, in the words of S. C. Hill, 'seldom of sufficient importance to be mentioned'. He makes exceptions for a few, men such as Govind Ram Mitra and Raja Naba Krishna, who prospered under the British and founded families of lasting wealth and influence. Hill hardly had high enough praise for the Bengalis, who he said were 'temperate and abstemious, charitable, ready to sacrifice their lives for the preservation of their religious purity, their women chaste and affectionate'. Not content with this description of these paragons, he quotes an earlier British writer who explained it further, and showed how religion and in particular the immutable fatalism of the caste system had its good points and its not so good, for a people who were 'almost strangers to many of those passions that form the pleasure and pain of our lives. Love – at least in the violent tumults of it – is unknown to the Gentoos [Hindus] by their marrying so young. Ambition is effectively restrained by their religion, which has by insurmountable barriers confined every individual to a limited sphere, and all those follies arising from debauchery are completely curbed by their abstaining from all intoxicating liquours. But,' he continued – there was bound to be a *but* – 'from hence also they are strangers to that vigor of mind and all the virtues grafted on those passions which animate our more active spirits . . .'

In other words, whether one viewed the Bengali character and customs as tending towards holiness or towards indolence, they were easy to dominate. And even without the coming of the hatmen, the Bengalis had a very choppy time of it in the eighteenth century. The new city at Murshidabad, strategically placed on the Hooghly, was founded by an opportunist convert to Islam named Murshid Kuli Khan (he modestly named the town after himself), who had managed to get the emperor to appoint him diwan, Delhi's financial representative. He had had to leave the Bengali capital at Dacca because he had quarrelled so badly with the nawab; he then set about giving a hard time to everyone else. He extracted huge sums from the foreign companies, including 25,000 rupees from the British to allow them to use the Royal Mint to coin their bullion; he is notorious for the destruction of Hindu temples in his town and miles around, apparently because he wanted to use their precious building materials for the construction of his own ostentatious tomb. Needless to say, he taxed the peasants mercilessly.

On his death his place was taken by his son-in-law, a Persian and a better man, by all accounts, who had in his retinue a pair of brothers called Ahmad and Alivardi Khan, also Turkoman Muslims. Alivardi started in some rather lowly capacity, but his story shows how with a bit of diplomatic skill, a lot of ambition and a complete absence of scruples, a modest start was no barrier, for Muslims, to making the kind of leap in position that was ruled out for the caste-bound Hindus. He made himself indispensable as a bold soldier, was given the governorship of some small, remote, troublesome part of the province, then cannily exploited a quarrel between the next (dissolute) diwan and the mighty and puritanical Seths, Hindus who had been appointed 'Merchants of the World'. In league with the Seths, he marched on the hopeless grandson of his early benefactor in Murshidabad, and claimed for himself the position of nawab.

Alivardi was treacherous but he was not cruel. It was considered positively odd that, when he conquered Murshidabad, he did not murder anyone, even to the extent of putting his rival's children under only 'gentle confinement'. This was almost as peculiar as the fact that he — according to Orme — 'had no pleasures and kept no Seraglio'. In other words, he had only one wife (potentates in his position usually main-

A view of Fort William from the Hooghly river, commissioned by the East India Company from George Lambert and William Scott in 1730, hung in the Court of Directors in London.

'The East offering her riches to Britannia', a painted ceiling panel that displays all the confidence of an armed trading company.

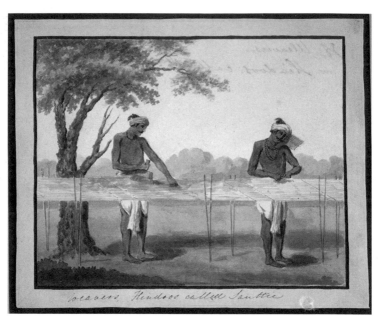

Above and below: Hindu weavers at work

The fashion for Eastern silks went from head to toe. Both men and women wore silk slippers and shoes, brocaded with metallic or silver thread and elaborately decorated. These were woven in Spitalfields, London, by weavers whose skills had come from the East centuries earlier.

A turban ornament, made in Bengal in the eighteenth century. Gold, with diamonds, rubies, a sapphire, an emerald and a large pearl: a typical gift from a grateful nawab to a helpful European. In the absence of a reliable banking system, valuables such as these were a practical way of transporting one's wealth.

The craze for Indian fabrics: in 1761, Captain John Foote of the East India Company chose to be painted by Sir Joshua Reynolds in Indian dress.

Siraj-ud-daulah was described by contemporaries as handsome and charismatic.

An idealized portrait of John Zephaniah Holwell, holding a design for the monument he erected to the victims of the Black Hole.

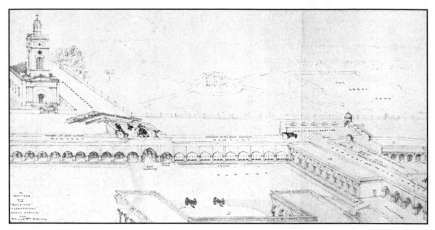

The parade ground of Fort William, showing the arcade with the Black Hole in the right-hand corner and St Ann's Church beyond the walls.

An imaginary view from inside the arcade: the Black Hole is behind the two closed arches on the left, with barred windows.

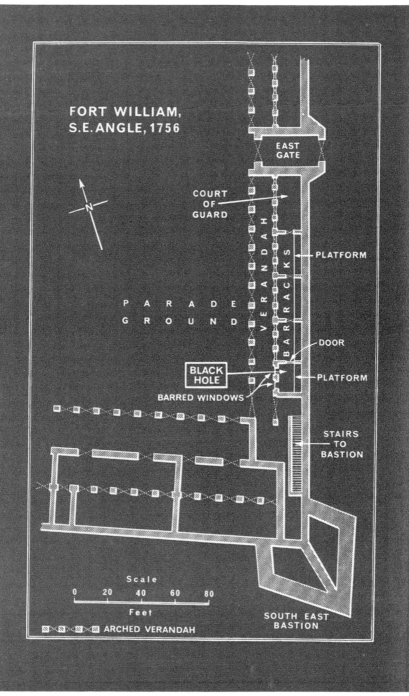

FORT WILLIAM,
S.E. ANGLE, 1756

N

COURT
OF
GUARD

EAST
GATE

PLATFORM

VERANDAH

BARRACKS

DOOR

PARADE

GROUND

BLACK
HOLE

PLATFORM

BARRED WINDOWS

STAIRS
TO
BASTION

Scale

0   20   40   60   80

Feet

ARCHED VERANDAH

SOUTH EAST
BASTION

The south-east corner of Fort William; the Black Hole is marked on the right.

J. Z. Holwell's original pukka-built monument to the Black Hole victims dominated views of Calcutta's centre, as did the larger replica erected by Lord Curzon.

This Monument
Has been erected by
Lord Curzon, Viceroy and Governor-General of India
In the year 1902
Upon the site
And in reproduction of the design
Of the original monument
To the memory of the 123 persons
Who perished in the Black Hole prison
Of old Fort William, on
On the night of the 20th of June 1756
The former memorial was raised by
Their surviving fellow-sufferer
J. Z. Holwell, Governor of Fort William,
On the spot where the bodies of the dead
Had been thrown into the ditch of the ravelin.
It was removed in 1821.

Lord Curzon's grander marble replica was moved from the site in 1940 in deference to nationalist feelings and now stands in an obscure corner of St John's Churchyard. Several decorative panels are engraved with names of victims, while this one tells the monument's story.

tained zenanas, or harems, of dozens or even hundreds of women) and stayed with her all his life even though she gave him no sons, only two daughters. Despite these eccentrically peaceful traits, his reign was almost as turbulent as his rise to power had been, with persistent attacks from the troublesome Marathas, which Alivardi fought off with 'dauntless courage, consummate military skill, and the most unscrupulous treachery'. He extracted huge sums of money from the foreign companies by pleading the expense of these wars and was otherwise rather strict with them, keeping them in line like naughty children and disliking any display of 'independence'.

For Alivardi, other enemies lurked closer to home, and the inevitable palace intrigues included a scheming rebellion in 1750 led by his own grandson, Mizra Mohammed, who became known as Siraj-ud-daulah, when the young prince was only twenty-one. Siraj was his grandchild and his great-nephew too, because Alivardi had married his two daughters to his brother's two sons. That had probably been a bad idea. The wild and reprobate boy – who was according to contemporaries 'remarkable for the beauty of his person' – was Alivardi's adored favourite, the son he never had, and the old man's extraordinary fondness for him survived even Siraj's open rebellion and many other less than attractive traits. Young noblemen of the provincial Mughal courts were utterly indulged, and knew almost no discipline, according to contemporary sources – the modern Muslim prohibitions against drink and drugs were not practised at the time, and the young Siraj was devoted to both. Even so, two years after the rebellion, Siraj was not only forgiven by his doting grandfather but was publicly declared his heir, despite a host of other contenders. Siraj set about getting rid of some of these, even before the throne was his, by what John Keay calls 'the usual bloodbath'. Siraj's own cousin, the Bengali historian Ghulam Hosein, left us the most damning assessment of the character of the heir apparent, who apparently made:

no distinction between vice and virtue, and paying no regard to the nearest relations, he carried defilement wherever he went, and, like a man alienated in his mind, he made the houses of men and women of distinction the scenes of his profligacy . . . and people on meeting him by chance used to say 'God save us from him'.

This is the man who would dream of driving the foreigners out of his territories, despite the massive wealth they generated for him, and almost immediately he got the throne launch an attack on Calcutta that would turn out to be so catastrophic. It was a move more idealistic than sensible, and it resulted, not least, in his own ignominious end.

There are those who claim that Siraj's many failings have been conveniently magnified by history – his casting as a cruel and crazy villain goes some way towards justifying the ruthlessness with which Clive arranged to have him deposed and dispatched by his own uncle, Mir Jaffir, after the battle of Plassey in 1757. Less than a year after he became nawab, in April of 1756, when he was just twenty-seven, Siraj ended his days in an ignominious death, apparently murdered by some of his own men, and the way was clear for Mir Jaffir to take control, as nawab, under the plan agreed with Clive. It was not a very British way of doing things, but it was very efficient. The level of Mir Jaffir's gratitude, and the nature of his relationship with the foreign interlopers, can be gauged by a glance into one of the display cases in London's V&A museum, which shows a turban jewel given by the new ruler to Admiral Watson, the commander of the naval forces at the battle of Plassey, as a token of appreciation. About ten inches in height and made of filigree gold, it contains a smooth sapphire of deepest blue about the size of a pigeon's egg, a glowing ruby and pearls that might have been laid by a whole flock of quails. It's an object of preposterous, outlandish richness and opulence; it puts many royal jewels in the shade. And as for Clive himself, his immense personal profit from the battle launched a thousand ships.

Whether Siraj was a villain or not, his attack on Calcutta was not really the action of a fully rational man, certainly not the action of an astute politician. Siraj had grown up with the example of his clever grandfather, who knew how to keep the foreigners under control and at the same time to make himself and many of his subjects vastly richer from the outsiders' trade. The remark for which Alivardi is most famous – that the foreigners in India were like hives of bees: you could take their honey, as much as you wanted, and they would continue to work away contentedly, but if you poked a stick into their hive they would come flying out and sting you to death – is the one Siraj might have listened to. But he obviously hadn't learnt the lessons well. Siraj hated the British, but he particularly hated Calcutta's difficult governor, Roger Drake, who seemed to take every opportunity to be tactless and obtuse. During the power-vacuum of Alivardi's long last illness, several of the British traders had overstepped the agreed limits on local taxes and local profits. The elaborate network of spies that the Murshidabad court employed within Calcutta and all the other trading settlements reported that both the British and the French were eyeing each other's factories and polishing their cannon, because of the outbreak of hostilities between their two countries far away in Europe.

Siraj became obsessed with the idea that the British were cheating him (they were) and increasing their fortifications (they weren't). Even so, even with some degree of provocation, to attack was not a wise idea. Perhaps the significant part of Hosein's character testimonial for Siraj may be the phrase 'like a man alienated in his mind'. There were other witnesses, too, who suggested not so much that Siraj was suffering from mental illness but that – according to the record left by a Calcutta merchant called Roger Scrafton – by Siraj's early twenties 'his mind was already affected' by drink and whatever else it was that the princeling was in the habit of ingesting.

Even the young man's wild habits had not altered Alivardi's decision about the succession, but he had gone so far – so the story goes – as to make Siraj swear an oath on the Koran never to drink again. Despite everything, Siraj is reputed to have kept his promise, though it made little difference. Perhaps the canny old man was realistic enough about Siraj's character to know that, by intrigue or murder or bribery or any other means, the young reprobate would manage to grab the throne anyway, so he might as well leave it to him. But he obviously had qualms. It may be with the wisdom of hindsight, but Ghulam Hosein claims that Alivardi once voiced his gloomy predictions 'in full company', saying that 'as soon as he himself should be dead, and Siraj-ud-daulah should succeed him, the hatmen would possess themselves of all the shores of India'.

If Alivardi really had this degree of prescience, he was remarkable. No western commentator seems to have had so much foresight, though after the event, in 1813, Charles Stewart, in *A History of Bengal*, summed Siraj's story up in a few tragic phrases:

The Nabob supposed that, from the capture of the Fort, and the destruction of the garrison, he [would have] rendered his government secure, and expelled the English from the country: whereas that very circumstance drew on him the vengeance of an inveterate foe, caused his death, and transferred the government to the hands of strangers.

7. The Heat of Battle

It is about 160 miles from Calcutta to Murshidabad, the Mughal provincial capital further up the Hooghly river. There were no roads between the two; it was almost impassable, swampy country; the river journey was unpredictable and tricky. Yet Siraj-ud-daulah's communications were remarkable. Through a system of spies and messengers, he seemed able to know what was going on in Calcutta in about thirty hours. And he was just as closely in touch with all the other forts and factories in his district: letters and messages, both official and secret, flew back and forth between the court and the French, the Dutch and the English, between the merchants who were the Mughal's intermediaries, to and from informers and agents in each place. And before the physical battle for Calcutta, there was a short, sharp war of letters.

It was a paper battle that the English could have won, with a little diplomatic skill. The older and more experienced Company men, like William Watts, who ran the smaller factory at Kassimbazar, up the river from Calcutta and only 12 miles from Murshidabad, knew that in Siraj they were dealing with a more dangerous character than his canny old grandfather Alivardi, who was doing much too well out of the foreigners to have any intention of trying to get rid of them. But Siraj, a hothead of twenty-seven with a taste for war and a special hatred for the English, needed more careful handling.

His animus against the British was probably caused by their powerful status in the trade wars. Some years earlier the British had managed – through a long and costly process of diplomacy and gift-giving – to extract a *farman*, or permission to trade, from the great Mughal himself in Delhi: this was a trump card that outranked anything the Bengal viceroys could produce. In one dispute after another, the British would close the argument by waiving the emperor's *farman*, a tactic that had enraged Alivardi and would infuriate Siraj even more. It even exempted the British from some of the endless local taxes and other demands that the nawabs could levy in Bengal. But some of the Company men exceeded its limits time and again, using it as a passport for private trade as well as the Company business for which it was intended. None of the other European companies had such royal backing, but each of them had learnt to negotiate their lesser privileges with skill. No one worried about the Danes, quietly getting on with their business at Serampore, and the Portuguese base at Bandel had been established for so long that they had almost the status of natives. The Dutch had no defences, and no pretensions to anything but trade, and used as their only resort the threat of leaving and taking away their lucrative businesses; the French were well liked by the Indian rulers, and – as S. C. Hill puts it rather pointedly – 'the Chiefs of *their* Settlements were able men'.

So that only left the British: too successful, too arrogant, too tactless, too well protected by Delhi, and showing all the signs of incipient expansionism. No wonder Siraj did not like them.

The year 1756 began badly. Alivardi was in his last long illness, and during Siraj's manoeuvres for the throne the heir apparent had dispatched almost all his many rivals – or at least those who might have challenged Alivardi's wishes after his death – with the exception of a cousin called Kissendas, or, in some versions, Khrishna Das. As the eldest son of Alivardi's daughter, Kissendas had just as much right to the throne as Siraj: here was a strong threat for the new prince.

Kissendas had no intention of waiting about to feel cold steel in his back, and as the old nawab lay dying, he announced that he and his wife were leaving on a pilgrimage to Orissa. Secretly, however, he had approached William Watts, at Kassimbazar, and asked him if he could stay in Calcutta for a while because his wife was expecting a baby. Watts was in a very difficult position: to refuse would seem churlish, perhaps even hostile, but to agree was very dangerous. As Noel Barber puts it: 'To give asylum, even temporary, to any contender for power was incredibly foolish, and the only charitable explanation for Watts's action is that his wife was also expecting a baby and he was moved by sympathy.'

Whatever the reason, Watts wrote to Drake in Calcutta to recommend that he should allow Kissendas to stay in the town – a letter he regretted soon afterwards, when he heard how angry it had made Siraj. It dawned on him that if the English seemed to be siding with Siraj's rival, it might be just the tipping-point for the bellicose young nawab-in-waiting. Before a few days were up, Watts was writing again, very urgently, to Drake, to implore him to get Kissendas out of Calcutta with all speed.

It was a bit late for that: Kissendas had moved his family and an impressive train of servants and retainers, rather ostentatiously, into Omichand's large house on The Avenue, in White Town. He had also apparently brought with him a large amount of treasure that had been removed from the court at Murshidabad – to the fury of Siraj. Omichand's motives here are slightly obscure. He was the consummate wily politician, skilled in the arcane ways of the Mughal courts. He must have known perfectly well what he was doing in extending this hospitality to Siraj's rival, and he must also have known what kind of trouble he would be bringing down on the British. Perhaps he too wanted to get rid of them and believed that it could be made to happen. It seems unlikely: he was a merchant, interested in his own wealth and in power of a purely financial kind. Yet he was not someone who would have acted without a long game in mind, and he had recently been badly treated by Drake, who had deprived him of some profitable business as an intermediary with the palace at Murshidabad – and Omichand, according to contemporary sources, was 'of a very vindictive temper'.

Holwell, a man of more experience and acumen, pleaded with the obstinate Drake to take Watts's advice and get rid of Kissendas and his retinue; other senior members of the settlement like Grant and even the Reverend Bellamy also tried to make the governor see reason, but without success. Whether Drake was stupid, whether his refusal was based on his evident delight in baiting Siraj, or whether he was just reluctant to cross the powerful Omichand (to whom he may have had all sorts of debts), we can't tell. But the strained relations in the Council chamber at Calcutta made everything worse: they could not decide, collectively, what to do; they squabbled and sniped at each other; they were as usual entirely self-obsessed and apparently quite unable to see what was about to happen.

Distant rumbles of larger trouble were reaching them from the outside world. Although there had not yet been a formal declaration of hostilities between the British and the French, what was to become the Seven Years War had already started, with fighting in various parts of Europe. In parts of the Indian continent, both sides began to look to their defences – previous conflicts with the French, ten years earlier in 1746, had caused some sharp fighting that ended with a brief English capitulation at Madras – but the Company men in Calcutta did very little. There was a vague attempt to restore the guns on the river side of the fort, but they would only be powerful enough, according to one visitor, to 'annoy' ships a little. The canny French in Chandernagore, not far up the Hooghly, decided on another form of attack. It may have been part of the national effort, it may just have been a regular bit of mischief, but they now saw a way to sow a little trouble for their powerful competitors. They made sure that Siraj's spies carried back to their master the 'news' that the British were preparing to pull up several warships and land a large contingent of soldiers primed to attack the French settlements. It wasn't true, but they had judged it just right: Siraj was more enraged than ever at the idea that the Europeans would contemplate carrying on their war in his country. Like Alivardi, he knew that in the south the political machinations of the French and the British had effectively reduced some local rulers to mere puppets: he was even more determined to deal with the hated British in his own backyard.

In the relationship between the nawabs and the British, it was not only on the Indian side that things had been building up, for some years now, to a fight. Robert Orme, the official historian of the time of the East India Company, and a confidant and acolyte of Robert Clive, gives some of the best analytical reports of the date. Not only are his comments detailed and accurate, but he was exceptionally well informed and clever. So when he warned Clive in 1752 that it might be time to take decisive military action, it was probably serious. In the letter to Clive on 25 August, what he said was:

the Nabob [Alivardi] coming down with all his Excellency's canon to Hughley, and with an intent to bully all the settlements out of a large sum of money; Clive, 'twould be a good deed to swinge the old dog. I don't speak at random when I say that the Company must think seriously of it, or 'twill not be worth their while to trade in Bengal.

Orme was not the only voice urging military action. As P. J. Marshall records, there were those in Leadenhall Street who were aware of the fundamentally inapposite basis on which the Company's possessions were held. The factories and cities had become too valuable and extensive to depend on the old system of royal favour, and royal bribes; the Company was 'either sovereign or at the mercy of a brutal and unpredictable tyrant'. There was no middle course. However, in Alivardi's time the balace of power held good, and the Company had not made any moves to 'swinge the old dog'. No need, according to the majority of the Court of Directors; regime change was hardly a priority when money was still to be made in such quantities. No need, according to the more fatalistic Indian view, since the next steps had in any case been arranged by a higher power. The historian Seer Mutakeen (Siraj's kinsman) explains that:

It having been decreed by Providence that the guilty race of Aly Verdi Khan should be deprived of an Empire that had cost so much toil in rearing, of course it was in its designs that the three provinces of Bengal, Behar and Orissa should be found to have for masters two young men equally proud, equally incapable, and equally cruel, Seradj-ed-doulah and Shaocat-djung.

Fate, or the logic of history and economics, or a series of fatal personality flaws – whatever one's belief, the next letters that issued from the palace at Murshidabad were a turning point. Within a few days of Alivardi's death on 10 April, Siraj wrote formally and fiercely to both the French and the English, ordering them peremptorily to pull down the new fortifications (never mind that there were none, in Calcutta at least). At Chandernagore, which was at this time a larger trading centre than Calcutta, the administrative system was different from that of the British East India Company. The French had a single governor for all their Indian possessions, and he was far away in the south, in Pondicherry. But in

Bengal a clever and bold military commander, Colonel Renault, had the wit that Governor Drake so clearly lacked. While Renault replied with dignity and courtesy to the messenger of the new ruler, Drake sent one of the stupidest and least-well-judged letters in this whole saga of stupidity and poor judgement.

The French simply placated Siraj-ud-daulah by telling him that they had only been repairing storm damage, and had built nothing new. It is likely that the nawab's ambassador would have returned to the court with a very nice present as well. Drake's petulant letter claims much the same – that the only work they were doing was a little maintenance – but it is so tactless that it even mentions the explosive subject of Europeans fighting each other on Indian soil. 'In the late War between our Nation and the French,' Drake wrote to Siraj,

they had attacked and taken the Town of Madras contrary to the neutrality we expected would have been preserved in the Mogull's Dominions; and that there being present great appearance of another War between the Two Crowns, We were under some apprehension they would act in the same way in Bengal, to prevent which We were only repairing our Line of Guns to the water-side.

Furious, Siraj did not dignify this missive with a direct reply. Instead he used one of the other accepted routes of communication and wrote to an Armenian merchant called Koja Wajid, who would have known full well that this was a message intended for the British. There could hardly have been a clearer warning. 'It has been my design to level the English fortifications raised within my jurisdiction on account of their great strength,' the nawab wrote. 'I shall use the utmost expedition in my march that I may arrive before Calcutta as soon as possible . . .' And in an angry postscript comes the battle-cry: 'I swear by the great God and the prophets that unless the English consent to fill up their Ditch and level their fortifications to the ground I will expel them from the country.'

The fact that Siraj used Koja Wajid as an intermediary for this declaration of war was probably another loop in the labyrinthine strategy: Siraj may have been somewhat crazy but he was not stupid. Wajid was a very important merchant and a substantial creditor of the French. Things had not been going well for the French Company, and they had large debts to the Seth family and to Wajid, as well as to many other money-lenders and merchants in the area: it was only Renault's personal credit that ensured cargoes for the French East India ships. Now Siraj obviously thought they would help him against the British, and Wajid obviously had a particular interest in making sure the French were not driven out of Bengal either through hostile action or through bankruptcy – otherwise the enormous sums they owed him would remain unpaid. In the event, the French did not help very much, and in a fit of pique Siraj fined them 300,000 rupees for their restraint, an amount that had to be provided by the long-suffering M. Renault.

Siraj's letter was written on 28 May: the message must have got through, but still no one in Calcutta did anything. Siraj was in no mood to wait. Within a few days, even the humblest Bengali peasant could hardly have failed to know what was going on: the size and might and noise of the army with which Siraj marched south razed a trail through the countryside. One French report – perhaps rather gleefully – describes the progress of a force so big that it took ten hours to pass by their factory.

In the lead were Siraj's crack troops, his cavalry. Eighteen thousand horsemen, fiercely armed and beautifully mounted, often led by their ruler himself, either on horseback, as he loved to be, or carried in his elaborate palanquin. Then came the infantry and the artillery with its cannon, and the huge animals that shoved and hauled the heavy guns over the wild ground: 500 elephants, decked with flags and bells and silks, each with its mahout and each specially trained for battle; horses and oxen and bullocks and mules, as many as several dozen pulling each of the cannon; 2,000 camels loaded with supplies. To lead this force, and to cope with the logistics of the terrain, Siraj had made use of foreign mercenaries: two Frenchmen who had been expelled from the fort at Chandernagore after a scandal had pitched their lot in with the nawab, and recruited others to join them. Jean-Baptiste Gentil, an army officer, was one of them, deputed to organize the progress of this vast force, while a clever strategist, the Marquis de St Jacques, had overall command of the artillery.

Then came the mob of common foot-soldiers, probably 30,000 of them, raggle-taggle and untrained but armed with anything they could get hold of – knives and spears as well as ancient muskets and swords. Finally, at the end, came the grim reapers of the countryside through which this army moved, 7,000 official looters, whose task it was to plunder and strip every village on the way in order to keep the great body of men and animals supplied with food and drink. The whole vast parade moved in a cacophony of drums and cymbals and rackety percussion that could be heard for miles. It has been difficult for historians to establish the real size of this force – estimates vary between 20,000 and 50,000 – but whatever the figures it would have been difficult not to know that they were coming.

The nawab's first stop was at Kassimbazar. William Watts found his small settlement surrounded at dawn on 24 May; the nawab's troops had also encircled the French and Dutch factories not far away. Since all the foreign factories were in the same position, Watts didn't realize, at first, that this attack was out of the usual run, and although he had no intention of making a stand, with his tiny force of just fifty men, he sent word to Calcutta for help – by which he meant that Drake should send the usual (money and respectful messages) to the nawab, in the usual way. Drake once again showed that he was one of those people who respond to a dilemma by doing nothing. To this message, and to the next, a far more alarmed one asking for military assistance, the Council at Calcutta made no response. When word finally arrived that the nawab's soldiers had withdrawn from the other foreign settlements but remained in a blockade around Kassimbazar, the story unfolded.

Watts had received word that the nawab wanted to see him. The troops had not been especially threatening, and had even allowed supplies into the factory, so Watts assumed that this meeting would be one of negotiation. But no – all the nawab did was curtly order his guards to arrest Watts, together with the fort's surgeon, Mr Forth, who had accompanied him. The two were held in chains; the garrison had no choice but to surrender. The terrified Mrs Watts, who was very close to having her baby, was allowed to take refuge with the French, and as the nawab's huge army resumed its march towards Calcutta on 5 June, Watts was carried along with them (perhaps as a hostage for bargaining purposes, perhaps as a potential source of information).

In these days and weeks of growing threat, Calcutta should have had time to prepare itself for attack. Drake had ordered some preparations for a siege, laying in food and sending orders to the military officers to ready the troops, and to Holwell to enlist buxerries, native gunmen. Letters went to Madras to ask for help. Drake had also written to both the Dutch and the French, asking if they could send some men and weapons, but neither was prepared to get involved in this dangerous quarrel, especially when they saw the nawab's huge forces march past Chinsura and Chandernagore on his way to confront the British. And although the Council had many more important things to do, they wasted some time writing back angry letters in reply to these refusals, especially to the French, whom they suspected of helping the nawab.

Not much had been done: the habitual lethargy and chaos reigned in the fort, and as the Council members tried to rouse themselves towards some sort of organization their discoveries went from bad to worse. In the Council chamber in the governor's house, a long, high room that ran the breadth of the building and commanded views out to the river beyond the walls, the ten most senior British officials dithered and delayed, avoiding until the last minute the truth that they had no defence plans at all. From that high room, the sight of the ships lying at anchor just beyond the fort must have been the only comfort. Not only were the walls of the fort almost useless – they had been pierced through with gateways at the ground level, and along the tops, where the cannon should have been supported, they were half rotted. The military commander, Minchin, had no idea how many guns they had, or what state they were in: fifty large cannon were traced to one of the wharves, still sitting where they had been unloaded from a ship three years earlier, but now rusted through and useless. Lieutenant Witherington, when asked about powder stocks, reported that there were copious amounts of gunpowder – but it was almost all damp. And as for the fighting men themselves, amazingly neither Minchin nor Clayton, his second in command, seemed to know how many there were, or even where they were. There should have been a garrison of about 300 in the fort, but some had been sent up to smaller stations in the area, some were unaccounted for, and it needed Surgeon Gray to inform the senior officers that no fewer than seventy European soldiers were in the hospital.

Governor Drake was now seriously alarmed: for the first time, it seems, he was beginning to realize what might be happening. When he could bring himself to speak to Minchin, a man with whom he had a long-running feud, he discovered that the available strength of defenders was just 180, including forty-five Europeans, mostly Dutch, and the rest mixed-race soldiers of various origins, or what one nineteenth-century source rudely dismisses as 'only portuguese'. A French officer, Lieutenant Lebeaume, was working for the British, and Drake now ordered him to form a committee, which he did by enlisting a trader called Simpson and the Company's chief engineer, the 24-year-old John O'Hara. The point of this committee was unclear, unless its job was to deliver one piece of bad news after another to the Council chamber. No shells. No fuses. No grapeshot that had not been eaten by worms. And as for the militia, a parade on 8 June still mustered a mere 250 men.

Messages went out to the captains of all the ships on the river, asking them to send their crews in to defend Calcutta, and some forty of them arrived – this is how Peter Carey came to be involved in the battle. The times were desperate, and 'many Company's servants and young gentlemen in the settlement entered as volunteers in the military, doing duty in every respect as common soldiers'; the other extras were Portuguese and Armenians (whom S. C. Hill describes as 'extremely awkward in the use of arms' and Holwell more roundly calls 'entirely useless') and 'black militia' (in Holwell's account 'boys and slaves not capable of holding a musket'). All in all, this motley crew came to 515 men, to defend the crumbling fortress against the nawab's tens of thousands. In the whole place there was only one officer, Captain Buchanan, who had ever seen any active service.

With the Company's passion for rank and protocol, a number of officers were appointed and given spurious military titles. Manningham and Frankland, two senior traders who were cronies of Drake, were dubbed colonel and lieutenant-colonel respectively, which made them senior to the military officers, even though they had no military experience. It was a sharp insult to Captain Minchin, Drake's enemy, who sulked furiously. 'This extraordinary arrangement,' writes Hill,

appears quite in keeping with the other ridiculous actions of the Council, and its only possible explanation is that the Council was so certain of repulsing the Nawab that its chief care was, under the pretence of not wishing to supersede senior military officers by their juniors, to make sure that none of the credit of the exploit should fall to the military.

In other words, even now they were playing politics and carrying on their petty rivalries. And even now they could not take in the reality of the situation.

When historians have looked back at the thousands of pages of detailed account that came out of the battle for Calcutta, one thing stands out. Despite the ridiculous disparity in numbers, despite a fort so feeble that men were now ordered to carry mattresses up out of one of the store rooms to buttress the walls, despite their lack of any sensible military command, these hatmen still did not believe that Indian troops could ever beat Europeans. To say they underestimated the nawab's army would be to put it mildly. They thought that their only real opponents were the French officers in the pay of Siraj; they didn't reckon with men like Roy Dulabh, one of the senior commanders of the nawab, skilled, astute and brave. It is true that the Indians had tens of thousands of ragged foot-soldiers whom they used more or less pitilessly as cannon-fodder, as well as the dreadful rabble of looters, but Dulabh also had 15,000 trained troops with a decade's experience of fighting the formidable Marathas. But for men like Minchin and his incompetent adjutant Clayton, as well as for Drake and many of the Council, these were all just natives.

How could they prevail against Europeans? A few pops of the cannon and they'd run away.

Admittedly, the illusion of European strength was one held not only by the Europeans. There were reports that the bulk of Siraj's army 'marched very unwilling', because they believed that to attack the Europeans meant certain death. These people seemed to be all-powerful.

This inability to face reality was tested more severely when John O'Hara, the engineer, presented the Council with his defence plan. He knew the problems better than anyone, because he had spent the last two years trying fruitlessly to get some support for projects to repair the fort and the Maratha ditch, but no one had wanted to pay the workforce.

When he had written a report the previous year warning of the town's vulnerability, the Council – including the newly minted colonel and lieutenant-colonel, Manningham and Frankland – had voted his letter 'irregular, improper and unnecessary'. So it may have given him some pleasure to announce to them now that there was only one way in which they could survive an attack. It was to abandon White Town altogether and defend only the fort itself, and to do this it would be necessary to demolish all the grand mansions that surrounded the walls. Because they were much higher than the fort, their great flat roofs and upper storeys would give a perfect platform from which the invaders could fire down into the fort itself. One of the largest and closest belonged to Mr Cruttenden, a member of Council, and it ran almost two-thirds of the length of the fort's north wall, towering above it. The streets and alleys that separated their gardens and compounds would give cover for the enemy to bring up their guns. If the houses were demolished, the defenders could fire down on to open ground: it was the only chance.

One can imagine the consternation in the Council chamber at this suggestion. To blow up their own houses, everything they'd earned and worked for and created in this God-forsaken place? It was unthinkable, and the only two sup-porters that O'Hara found were Holwell and Captain Grant (whose houses, admittedly, were not very close to the fort and might therefore have been spared). Holwell tried to broker a compromise by suggesting that if the houses stayed standing, the British forces should occupy them strategically – this too was vetoed. Grant wrote afterwards that 'so little credit was then given, and even to the very last day, that the Nabob would venture to attack us . . . that it caused a general grumbling and discontent'. That was probably an understate-ment. It caused outrage and anger and absolute denial. There was still a faint hope of a settlement, too. When Koja Wajid's diwan brought the British the letters from Siraj to his master, Wajid's advice had been to prepare for an attack. But as he also told them that he was going to meet the nawab, they were hoping that he would negotiate for them; meanwhile, a letter also arrived on 12 June from the redoubtable William Watts, a prisoner with the nawab's forces, saying that there was still a chance of sending someone to Siraj's camp with a suitable pay-off.

The intrigues and machinations were still going on, in a flurry of letters. Koja Wajid had warned the British against Omichand, who he said had encouraged Siraj to launch the attack, as a revenge on them for curtailing his financial activi-ties. It had been suspected by some that the whole issue of Kissendas had in fact been a ploy, to trick the British into harbouring someone who was apparently an opponent of the nawab and then to use that as an excuse for attacking the town. (The fact that after the capture of Calcutta Kissendas was awarded an honour rather bears this out.) Drake decided to imprison both Omichand and Kissendas – the first to prevent any further trouble-making on his part, the latter as a bargaining counter – and these two unfortunates were put into the Black Hole. But Watts' letter contained a warning against Wajid, whom he believed to be the man responsible for setting Siraj against the British, rather than Omichand. There was a letter from the ubiquitous Marquis de St Jacques, offering to negotiate between the British and the nawab, but M. Renault at Chandernagore warned against trusting him. At the same time informers reported that St Jacques had been to the French asking for supplies, and that he had got stocks of gunpowder from them – so it wasn't clear that Renault was to be trusted either. A letter went out from the Catholic bishop of Calcutta to the French and Portuguese in charge of the nawab's artillery, remonstrating with them as Christians for taking the side of a Muslim against other Christians. And then Wajid – whom the Council was forced to rely on, despite their suspicions – put forward another offer, that Omichand should be sent to talk to Siraj – but this was interpreted as a ploy to get him out of prison and out of the town.

There was still some hope of help from Madras. Another decisive force, too, might weigh in: the monsoon, if it arrived in time, would not only stop Siraj literally in his tracks but make fighting impossible. It was only a matter of days.

When Omichand was imprisoned, a terrible thing took place. Obviously fearing for the fate of his wives and children if there was an attack when he was not there to protect them, or if one or other faction won, he left instructions with his trusty Jamadar about his harem. As soon as Omichand had departed with the soldiers who had come to arrest him, the servant led thirteen women and three children into the coconut grove at the back of his master's house and killed them all, stabbing each one in the chest, waiting for the next to step forward submissively as the last one fell to the ground.

It was an appalling and extreme reaction, but it gives some idea of the panic that was beginning to grip Calcutta. There was no thought of trying to defend Black Town, and as the rumours and reports swirled around the bazaars the inhabitants knew that they would have to fend for themselves. While the Company men dithered and bickered up in the fort, the residents of Black Town were streaming out of the city in their thousands, heading for the countryside, anywhere that presented a chance of safety. They knew what was coming. The nawab had issued orders that no shopkeepers or merchants were to supply the British, on pain of his displeasure and its consequences, so whether Black Town's inhabitants were more afraid of the hatmen or the incoming forces was not clear, but as many as 80,000 fled. The British raised the pay of all their native workers, desperate to keep the labour force they needed, huge squads of coolies to dig defences, destroy bridges across the Maratha ditch and raise hastily constructed barriers and palisades under the energetic command of John O'Hara.

Now an eerie silence fell on White Town, too: the servants left. As if at a silent command, one morning they were simply gone. The streets were suddenly empty of the bustle of normal life – the guards, the cooks and maids going to and from the bazaar, the boys who ran errands and held umbrellas over white heads against the sun, the bearers of palanquins and the carriage drivers. There had been so many of them: the widowed Lady Russell, alone in her mansion at the edge of White Town, had kept four servants whose sole job was to swat flies. But now the huge houses echoed emptily, and the white women were faced for the first time with the idea that they might have to cook and shop and keep house, although most probably had no idea how to do so. 'It is ironic to reflect,' Noel Barber says, 'that it was the defection of their servants rather than any other factor which suddenly roused the inhabitants of Calcutta to an acute realization that urgent measures were a necessity for survival.'

The women did not have long to worry about their houses,

however. On 15 June all the European families were told to abandon their homes and move into the fort, with their children and a few possessions, for safety.

Siraj's army, which was now augmented by guns and ammunition taken from Kassimbazar, had moved with speed, and covered the distance from Murshidabad in only eleven days. The monsoon had not broken; he was in luck. On 12 June a forward party of his soldiers had been spotted at Dum-Dum, where Calcutta's airport is today; by the next day, a larger force was just 15 miles to the north of the town. Another day went by, and the flickering lights of fires and the incessant drums could be seen and heard from the fort itself: Siraj and his army were just the other side of the Maratha ditch.

Through the intense heat of the last few days, when the thermometer rarely dropped below 100, even at night, the British in their fort had finally moved into a frenzy of activity. Women made cartridges and stuffed cotton sacks to buttress the parapets and checked stores of food and medicines; men did the best they could with the sagging walls and rusty weapons; all the native labour force that could still be mustered with the lure of triple pay dug defences that criss-crossed The Park. The children fretted and cried in the sweltering heat, and the tiny airless rooms of Writer's Row were now so crowded with the British families that the stench of overflowing latrines began to fill the building. But there was, at last, a plan. Six groups were formed out of the small force available: one to guard the fort itself, three to man the batteries that had been strategically set up, one as reserve. And one, led by a 24-year-old ensign called Piccard, helped by Peter Carey (who was probably about the same age) and a clerk-volunteer called Ralph Thoresby, aged twenty-three, that was ordered to take twenty men to Perrin's Redoubt, a small pukka-built guardhouse on the northern edge of Calcutta, a couple of miles from the fort, where the dilapidated Chitpur bridge had once crossed the Maratha ditch.

On the night of 15 June, informers had brought Drake the news that this was the place where Siraj had decided to launch his assault, at dawn the next day, and there was no secret about his preparations. In the jungle on the far side of the ditch the great animals crashed through the undergrowth, hauling and shoving the huge cannon; the fires of 4,000 men gave glimpses of the camps half-hidden in the trees; the drums kept up their rhythm. An attack at this point along the ditch was a bizarre decision, and one that historians still cannot fully explain. Here was one of the few places where the ditch was actually a serious obstacle, 12 feet wide and about 15 deep, hard to negotiate even for a lithe Bengali, impassable for heavy guns and the animals who moved them. Along most of its length the ditch was much smaller, and everyone knew that it was actually unfinished, and that there were places to the south where all the nawab's elephants could simply have plodded into White Town. Why didn't the nawab, with all his spies and informers, know that? There were many places along the ditch that were impossible to defend – why attack at the one place where there was a proper guardhouse with gun emplacements? And if Roy Dulabh was as astute as reports make him out to be, why did he risk so many men on this pointless assault?

It was a strategy so strange that one commentator, Iris MacFarlane, takes it as evidence that the battle for Calcutta was a fixed match. She believes that Dulabh – who could even have been in league with the British – deliberately misled his ruler about the nature of the place, thinking that after this first bloodbath Siraj would get disheartened and make a truce.

Whether or not that is true, the battle took place. It was one of those things of which legends are made: twenty-four defenders, three very young and inexperienced Europeans with their assorted mixed-race soldiers and twenty-two mus-kets between them, facing the 4,000 Bengalis. They had some back-up from the *Prince George*, a ship that had been ordered to move up the river and train its big guns on the ditch, but apart from that they were alone. They had been told to expect no reinforcements before noon.

They waited. Dawn came, and with it the first surprise. The sun came up and the heat started to build, but there was silence from the opposing camps. This was odd: Indians fought in a formal and predictable way, always attacking at dawn and always stopping on the stroke of twelve, whatever the state of play, and resting through the midday heat until three o'clock. The fighting would then resume, until sunset, when quiet would abruptly fall again. It was as ordered as a football match, and opponents who did not observe the rules were considered very uncouth.

This time, Dulabh had decided to unnerve the defenders by making them wait. The heat had already become almost intolerable, and the guns too hot to touch, when at ten o'clock the war of nerves took a new and horrible turn: a single loud wail was heard from the jungle, a sustained high shriek that was echoed by another voice, then another and another, until suddenly the jungle wall became a great line of screaming men, advancing in their hundreds in a rank 200 yards wide, armed with sabres, scimitars, bayonets and muskets.

The accounts of the first battle make exciting reading. How the musket fire blazed and cracked out from the British in the guardhouse, picking off the Indians like nine-pins, wave after wave of them rushing out of the trees towards the ditch but falling back in a pile of bodies, until suddenly St Jacques' cannon roared out of the jungle and smashed into the defenders' fragile fortress, killing and wounding some of their small number. How the renewed assault by the Indians seemed about to overwhelm them by sheer force of numbers as they frantically reloaded and fired again, sluicing their weapons with water to cool them, until the gunners from the *Prince George* located the cannon-flashes of the enemy and a mighty shot from the river flashed past the guardhouse and exploded beside the ditch in a horrific cloud of blood and body parts and corpses falling like ragdolls to join the heap in the ravine. And how they just kept coming anyway, so many that the Europeans were fighting hand-to-hand around their defence, until Piccard coolly chose his moment to fire his big guns into the mob of advancing troops only 50 feet away. And then, suddenly, the flood of invaders faltered and slowed, and started to turn back, now trying to use the ditch as shelter from the ship's cannon. There were other assaults before noon, other hits from the Indian cannon and other losses, but none so desperate. When the break came at noon and the wheeling vultures gathered to the bodies already swelling and reeking in the heat, Piccard and Carey saw that Ralph Thoresby had been killed, the first casualty among the Company's staff, together with about four soldiers of their small force. Four more, as well as Piccard himself, were wounded.

The day wasn't over, however. The exhausted men were woken from a noon-time sleep by a messenger from the fort, where for once a little strategic thinking was taking place. Holwell and Grant had persuaded Drake to think laterally, and send the 21-year-old Lieutenant Blagg with fifty men and three large guns to take up a position in the bazaar, from where they could fire on the attackers from yet another angle. They had started two hours earlier, since it would take so long to move the cannon, with whatever oxen and horses they could find, even a mile or two – the largest gun weighed 27 tons. The plan was that at 2.15 p.m. precisely, the *Prince George*, Lieutenant Bragg and Piccard's men should take on the Indians from three sides.

It was carnage. A lucky hit knocked out two of the nawab's

cannon and killed three of the French officers; the common troops were so terrified, after the bloodbath of the morning, that most refused to budge. There is a description of two elephants that broke their chains and ran amok, trumpeting in terror as they charged out of the jungle and tumbled crazily into the ditch – but this sounds like an embellishment. With fire from three angles, the Indians turned and bolted. Later, the nawab admitted that 800 of his men had lost their lives.

It was the first strike, and a brilliant success. Coordination and planning, as well as almost unbelievable courage, had meant that the British had won out against astonishing odds. It was the last time that an action was so well planned. It had also been completely pointless. The invaders had lost hundreds of men to gain nothing, and the British had defended nothing – even as the battle was still under way, a mile or so along the ditch to the east the bulk of Siraj's forces were already erecting a vast city of tents centred on the garden belonging to Omichand, not the large house on The Avenue but his summer house on the outskirts, which Siraj had chosen for his own headquarters. It stood inside the line of the ditch. It had not taken them long to find out how easy it was to cross over at a makeshift bridge at Cow Cross, on the Dum-Dum road. The story has it that it was Omichand's faithful servant who, though badly wounded, had rushed to the nawab in the night with a letter carrying the information that this famous ditch was not the formidable barrier he believed it to be, but this must be apocryphal. Just about anyone who had ever been to the town could have told him that. Omichand may have saved him the trouble of a bit of recce, though, if it was he who confirmed that there was a crossing big enough to take all his troops and guns and animals, due east of the fort, on a long, straight road that was the continuation of The Avenue. The British called it the Bread and Cheese Bungalow.

The next day was a Thursday. It was the fasting month of

Ramadan, which the nawab observed carefully, and he decided to plan his big attack for the following day, a Friday that corresponded to 19 Ramazan in the Muslim calendar, a day considered auspicious. Siraj and his commanders made so little secret of their plans that it hardly needed the usual informers to scuttle to the fort with messages for the Council. All through that Thursday, the Indian troops moved into position behind the Bread and Cheese Bungalow with as much noise as they wanted, and with no attempt to hide their cannon or the trains of pack-camels bearing ammunition. By now the nawab's magnificent camp stretched halfway to the horizon out of the town to the east, just a mile or two from the fort, and although the thousands of common soldiers had more or less to fend for themselves in the open air, for the officers there were brilliantly coloured and ornamented tents in lines running up to the central point, the nawab's own huge headquarters, 60 feet long, festooned in gold and scarlet silk and richly carpeted. Here he was waited on by 100 personal servants and a dozen cooks, who prepared gleaming delicacies for him and his favourite officers, and guarded by armed and splendidly uniformed soldiers; pomp and circumstance were all-important. Among the officers both Hindus and Christians were well catered for in their lavish tents, the French apparently provided with barrels of wine and 'a complement of unattached ladies'. Discipline was tight, though, and the nawab's every whim was treated as if it were holy writ. Apart from anything else, it was well known that Siraj especially hated being woken up when he was asleep, at whatever time of day, and anyone who did so was quite likely to lose their nose and ears.

This graceful living was a stark contrast to what was going on inside Fort William. There the formal wigs and waistcoats, the lace and brocade, had already been abandoned; the grim conditions, the overcrowding and the heat had already brought on the first cases of dysentery. Water was scarce, so even in the relentless heat men and women went unwashed. There was no bedding except for the sick and wounded, and Ann Mackett and Sarah Mapletoft, both of whom were about to give birth, had only a little straw to lie on, and hardly the strength to shoo away the mosquitoes and the rats. There is a kind of flying beetle called a bugfly, which now invaded the fort, settling on every surface, on children's faces. It has a rank smell like that of a skunk. It is at about this point, in some of the records, that Mary Carey makes her appearance. She comes as a bright and capable presence, almost an angel of mercy, kind and patient with the children, long-suffering and brave in dealing with the wounded, a tireless worker when there were meals to be cooked, bandages to be washed, cartridges to be filled and cotton-bags to be stuffed. In a story so short of heroes, she may be the heroine we crave.

But where did she come from, and why was she there? Her husband Peter was fighting with the British, certainly. His presence is well recorded – and on the night before going off to defend Perrin's Redoubt with Ensign Piccard and the unfortunate Ralph Thoresby, he is supposed to have gone to the kind old Reverend Bellamy, who had taken refuge in the fort with his wife and daughter, to ask him to look after Mary if he should not return, and in particular to make sure that she would be included if the European women and children were evacuated to safety. But Peter was of a very lowly rank, a simple seaman, and there were many non-European residents of Calcutta who were far more prominent and wealthy than Mary who were not offered the protection of the fort. Govind Ram Mitra, for example, a Bengali merchant as important as Omichand but less duplicitous, had a summer garden immediately adjoining that of his better-known counterpart: it must have been commandeered by Siraj for his camp, and Mitra himself was imprisoned by the nawab's new governor of Calcutta immediately after the battle was over. It was bad luck on him – but although the British had needed him all these years, he was not part of their plans when it came to saving people's skins.

The most likely explanation for Mary's presence in the fort is that she was working for one of the Company families, perhaps as a children's nanny or governess, and had come into the fort with them. Otherwise, from her modest house on the divide between Black Town and White Town, if that was where she lived, she would never have been part of the general call for refuge. Anyway, where was her mother? 'Eleanor Weston', the only woman who appears in the inscription on Lord Curzon's Black Hole monument, was, Mary claimed in old age, her mother – but her mother was almost certainly Indian and therefore probably not called Eleanor. And Mary also claimed a ten-year-old sister with her in the Black Hole – if this was true, no one noticed. What's more, when Mary married again, after the fall of Calcutta and Peter's death, her new husband's name was Weston, so it is most likely that the woman named on Curzon's monument is in fact Mary Carey in another guise.

The more you look at her, the more mysterious and spectre-like she becomes. A cross between Florence Nightingale and the Angel of Mons, she appears in none of the first accounts, but neither do any of the other women. The role in which she is most often cast, in the drama of Fort William, is as a comforter and shepherd to the small band of frightened European children, along with Anna Bellamy, the daughter of the Reverend, and the redoubtable Lady Russell.

A Mary-figure was badly needed in the Fort on 17 June – things were about to go from very bad to much worse. That evening, after dark, an orangey glow slowly began to light up the velvet night sky. Calls and shouts faintly reached the fort; smoke began to stray across the evening air. Captain Tooke, on guard that night, surveyed the view from the highest eastern point of the fort and saw a sight that made his blood run cold: looking across to Black Town he could see that the bazaar was alight, the flames crackling higher and wilder every moment, set by a wild mob of thousands of the nawab's looters, who were rushing greedily down every alley and passageway of the labyrinthine settlement grabbing and grasping, taking what they wanted and torching the rest, turning people out of their shops and houses, hacking them down like weeds. The wooden houses went up like tinder, their inhabitants running out half-dressed and desperate; the cruder mud shanty dwellings were more or less crushed in the onslaught. The looters were looking for money and treasure, above all: anyone who looked at all prosperous was violently manhandled and threatened into giving up their wealth.

The town was put to the torch; quickly, in that heat, everything went to the flames. A tide of distressed and desperate people flowed everywhere in utter confusion and terror, some out towards the relative safety of the countryside beyond the ditch, but others inwards, towards White Town and the fort. Among those who fled were almost all the coolies still employed by the British: at least 1,000 of them evaporated away that night. But those who turned to the fort were soon at the east gate, hundreds of women and children and old people, begging for asylum in the place where their menfolk were. These were the families of the 'black militia' fighting with the British, and they had nowhere else to go. The guards on duty at the gate tried to close it on them, but found themselves challenged at knifepoint from inside the walls: if their wives and children were not taken in to safety, the native soldiers insisted, they would refuse to fight. The gate was pushed open; the refugees streamed into the fort, on to the parade ground and into any shelter they could find.

At a rough estimate, about 2,000 women and children and

old people forced their way into Fort William that night. They were not only the poor families of soldiers: there were tradespeople and even wealthier merchants who had managed to leave Black Town with servants and provisions, who proceeded to live and eat and cook and sleep in the open surrounded by their retinue as if they were still at home. But most of the incomers were poor to start with, and even poorer now that they had had to run from the fire leaving everything behind. The next morning, as Calcutta's men faced the battle for their survival, they could hardly walk across the parade ground that had been so spacious and pristine for the sheer press of people, sitting, squatting, lying down, making tiny fires to boil a few grains of rice, keening with head in hands or curled up asleep with their children fiercely clutched to them.

There was one more heroic stand in the fight against the nawab. The east battery, closest to the Bread and Cheese Bungalow where Siraj's army was clustered, was commanded by the idiotic Captain Clayton, for the sole reason that Manningham so disliked him he had sent him out of the fort, when others had argued for the command to go to Holwell. Holwell had to be content with second in command, alongside the Frenchman Lieutenant Lebeaume and the English Ensign Carstairs. They fought boldly and cleverly, with a particularly audacious plan carried out by Lebeaume that involved holding the gaol to prevent the Indians getting any further down The Avenue towards the fort.

It was almost like Piccard's stand at Perrin's Redoubt: the British side was outnumbered by hundreds to one. But this time there was no back-up from ships at anchor, or from heavy guns placed to their side. All they could do was hold out, for many hours, against the waves on waves of Indian troops who rushed towards them.

Unbelievable as it sounds, in the Council chamber, the senior men were still bickering and dithering. Minchin was all for turning the native refugees out of the fort, even though it would alienate the very troops he was meant to be commanding. Frankland proposed that the fort should be completely evacuated; Manningham wanted to evacuate only the women and children. Drake, as usual, could not make a decision. Minchin was still stoutly of the belief that the nawab was bluffing and would not attack the fort – if he had been at the east battery with Holwell and Lebeaume and Carstairs he might have thought it an odd kind of bluff. It wasn't going well there: despite everything they could do against the invaders, it was not long before the nawab's flag was hoisted on the roof of Lady Russell's house, and – just as John O'Hara had predicted – the Indians began to slip invisibly through the lanes and alleys at the back of the large houses and occupy them one after the other. No sooner had the British fought back and driven the Indians out of one than another was occupied, and Siraj's pennant flew from one rooftop after another, arrogant and triumphant.

The fighting ebbed and flowed around the White Town, half heroic, half blundering. Lieutenant Blagg made a magnificent stand in – ironically – the house belonging to Captain Minchin; when he was finally trapped it was Henry Lushington who came to his aid. Carey was there, and according to most reports survived the bloody encounter, although in some commentaries he is listed as having died in the defence of the place. Lebeaume was missing, after a furious argument in which he had accused Clayton of cowardice; Holwell had galloped back to the Council chamber to beg for reinforcements. Very young men, barely in their twenties, who had never held a gun before except to pot at duck or snipe on the banks of the Hooghly, had been pitched into this fierce battle; many of them did not come out. Meanwhile, St Jacques' cannon, pulled further and further towards the fort as the British were beaten back, had found their range and blazed out a series of massive shots that had whistled over the walls and down into the centre of open parade ground, scattering the unprotected children and women in a hellish pandemonium of blood and death.

8. The Black Hole

All this time, as many as twenty ships of various sorts were quietly sitting at anchor on the river, just outside the fort. From the tops of the walls you could see them clearly. As well as the big ships there was a small armada of little boats, used for short trips or for ferrying passengers and bundles out to the ships; one of the most usual was the local wide flat-bottomed *budgerow*. They might have seemed comforting, a reliable final escape route, but it wasn't necessarily so. If they fled on the ships, the British would be saying a final goodbye to everything they had owned and had worked for; anyway, where would they go? Beyond the immediate bounds of the town, the country was hostile and the banks of the river presented few friendly landing-places. To perch for a while as rather unwelcome guests at another European fort was the best they could hope for. And then what? England was months away, unattainable.

Yet even if there were these psychological barriers to a retreat by river, and practical ones too, it is amazing that no plans had been made to evacuate the fort. It was obviously getting very urgent to provide a safe route out for the women and children, at least. For a day or so, two of the senior Company men, Manningham and Frankland, had been suggesting the *Dodaldy*, which was lying conveniently close by, ready to sail. They could board the European families and send them down the river to the Dutch settlement at Fulta, nearer the delta of the Hooghly, where they would be likely to receive a welcome.

It appeared to be a generous offer. Conveniently, these

two happened to be joint owners of the *Dodaldy*. Much more likely, though, was that the pair were anxious about their investment and eager to get their ship well out of the way of the nawab's fire-arrows, which were fired from the shore or from smaller boats that crept up on the big ships to set them alight. After a bit of wrangling Drake agreed, but insisted that the departure should take place secretly and under cover of darkness. If the terrified hundreds huddled in the parade ground realized that the Europeans were starting to leave, there would be panic; if the local soldiers suspected that white women were being taken to safety while their families remained, they would lay down their guns and refuse to fight.

The women and children could slip out of Writer's Row and through one of the gates on to the river without crossing the parade ground, and that night, soon after dark, they filed down to the budgerows that would ferry them out to the ship: Sarah Mapletoft with her tiny girl, who had been born the previous day, Ann Mackett wrapped in a blanket and carried to the boat because she was too weak to walk after suffering a miscarriage. Although this evacuation became one of the most controversial events of all, raked over time and again in the bitter recriminations that came later, all we know for sure is that in the darkness and confusion most of the women managed to get on board the *Dodaldy*, but some were left behind – including the governor's unpopular wife, Mrs Drake, and Lady Russell – to be evacuated the following day.

Both Manningham and Frankland had volunteered to supervise the safe boarding and departure of the families – and to guard against a rush from any unwanted passengers. Just to make sure that all was well, they each went out to the anchored ship on the small boats carrying the women and children, and Manningham claimed later that since no soldiers had been sent as bodyguards, he felt he had to stay with them. In fact, neither of the men had any intention of returning.

'Our Colonel and Lieutenant-Colonel of militia,' wrote a bitter eye-witness, 'preferred entering the list under the number of women rather than defend the Company's and their own property. Accordingly they went off with them, and though several messages were sent them . . . no persuasion could avail.' Two militia officers, Wedderburn and Holmes, were sent to board the *Dodaldy* with messages from Governor Drake demanding their return – the ship had not yet sailed, only moved some way down the river – but they returned empty-handed.

So much attention was paid by later writers to this stark desertion that the details of the women who left are not very clearly recorded. It is at this point that accounts vary about what happened to Mary Carey. One list names thirty-two children and fifty women, including a 'Miss Cary', who eventually sailed safely down to Fulta. In another version, dramatically recounted by Noel Barber, Mary was ready at the ghats that night, about to shepherd half a dozen frightened children on to the boats, when the vigilant Manningham rudely barred her way and flatly refused to allow her aboard. Lady Russell – not a woman who was used to being crossed – took Mary's side in an angry scene on the dark river bank, but Manningham would not budge. It was because of her race: he would allow only white women on board, and he claimed that if Mary were to join them then it would set an impossible precedent for all the other women of different races huddled in the fort.

Even more dramatically, Barber follows this with a terrible scene that unfolded later on board the *Dodaldy*. By coincidence, it was the ship on which Peter Carey was serving before he was seconded to fight for the fort. That night he rowed out to the ship, presumably to say goodbye to Mary, since he assumed she was on board. When he discovered that she wasn't there and heard what had happened, he stormed

138

into the grand cabins demanding to see Manningham and the captain, a hard Scotsman called Andrew Young, for an explanation. Shouting was heard, and the furious Young pulled a pistol on Carey, who escaped by diving off the ship and swimming to shore.

This is surely part of the 'lightly fictionalised' element of Barber's book. Carey was an ordinary seaman; even in these extraordinary times, he would not have dared to make a scene in front of the captain and the ship's owner. His punishment would have been a flogging he might not survive. But it makes a dramatic tale.

According to this version of events, Manningham's appalling bigotry was the reason why Mary was left behind when all the other women went, and why she found herself incarcerated in the Black Hole two days later with the remaining defenders of the fort. The trouble is that this doesn't quite make sense. Several authorities record that other women were left behind that first night, because the ships were too full and the boarding so chaotic, but they all left on other boats the next day. So even if Manningham had been ruthless towards Mary, she could simply have gone on another sailing. Anyway, by then he himself had left. Other men went too – Holwell is supposed to have sent some women off on the *Diligence*, of which he was part-owner, with Lieutenant Lebeaume, who had been seriously wounded in the fighting, and by the next day as many ships as could be pressed into service were leaving Calcutta.

So if Mary was among those locked up in the Black Hole, she may have chosen to stay behind. Her husband was there, still alive and miraculously unwounded through all the fierce fighting in which he had taken part. And somewhere in the ruins of Black Town, or even among the mob on the parade ground, may have been her mother and others of her family. Calcutta was her home, not a distant outpost as it was for the other wives, and she may have preferred to take her chances on leaving the fort alive and picking up the pieces of her old life to being marooned with a lot of older foreign women in a distant Dutch settlement with no money, no family and no way of getting back.

Late into the night of 18 June, the British sat in the Council chamber discussing what to do next. As usual, it was a muddle: there was much talk about a general evacuation the following day, but no proper plans were made. The atmosphere in the fort was getting more and more tense, and the next morning it was even worse. There was very little food for the men, who had lived through the siege on nothing but hard biscuit, because all the cooks had run away, and although there were plentiful supplies of rice and wheat no one had remembered to lay in any cooking pots. The mercenaries had found alcohol in the fort, however: now perpetually drunk, sometimes violent and increasingly mulish, they were close to being out of control. Some had to be forced to fight at gunpoint, some deserted to the nawab, some made trouble among the young Indian women sheltering in the fort. Two Dutchmen were shot for looting. It was almost impossible for the British to fight any more.

The nawab's forces were very close now, surrounding the fort and firing constantly in on the terrified refugees and the dispirited troops. The prediction about the high houses around the walls turned out to be quite right – you couldn't even stand upright or walk around the walls now without making yourself a target for the enemy snipers so close by on their vantage points. They had begun to break their own convention about fighting after dark, too, and that night some of the nawab's soldiers were discovered trying to scale the walls of the fort with ladders across the warehouses built against the southern part. The call to arms went out inside the fort, but the exhausted and mutinous soldiers did not even respond: 'not a man could be brought on the ramparts,' Captain Grant wrote, 'till dragged from the different corners of the Fort where they had retired to rest'. On the parade ground there was trouble too; most of the refugees were hungry and thirsty as well as frightened, and it was impossible to stop the fights of panicked, starving people. There was chaos everywhere, the outposts were barely holding out against the enemy, and Governor Drake was at the end of his tether.

The enemy's bombardment started up again at first light, pounding the fort harder than ever. It had eventually been decided by the Council that a retreat to the boats would be organized that night, and the news had brought some spirits back to the exhausted men. But something overheard by chance threw all the plans into chaos. Lieutenant Witherington, the officer in charge of munitions, thought he was speaking privately when he broke the terrible news to Drake that the stores of dry powder were almost empty: there was no more. Somehow, they were overheard by some of the Portuguese women, who understood enough of what had been said to spread around the parade ground the news that the fort could not fight any more. There was 'utmost horror' among the women, whose only thought was to get themselves and their children away. They had seen Black Town burn, and they knew what was likely to happen to them if the nawab's looters swarmed into the fort itself. A huge crowd surged in panic to the back gate that led to the waterside, and began to pack themselves into any boats they could find along the shore, in one case as many as 200 people and children in a boat made to hold forty. They managed to push off, and the boat began to float downstream; suddenly, under the horrified gaze of the soldiers on the ramparts, who could do nothing, a stream of fire-arrows came from the Indians in Cruttenden's house, overlooking the ghats, and in a moment the boat was alight. Dozens of women, their clothes on fire, leapt into the swirling currents of the river only a few moments before the whole boat lurched and sank: 'those who were eye-witnesses of this confusion,' wrote one, 'counted the number they saw drowned at more than two hundred people'.

It was another horrible incident caused by the chaos of the situation, and it seemed to have a deep effect on the men who witnessed it. Still smarting from the shock of Manningham and Frankland's desertion, they must have felt this new horror as some kind of turning point. In a rousing letter to the Company directors in London, Holwell later described the defection of the two senior traders, and their refusal to come back to the fort even for a discussion in Council, as:

the primary causes of all the confusion that ensued . . . had we remained united in our forces, and proper spirit shewn and examples made, what could have been apprehended from a few drunken Dutch soldiers or a few seditious among the rabble of the militia? [We] were surely more than equal to quell any tumult that could have been raised.

But the 'proper spirit' was sadly lacking. What's more, just at the same moment as the panicking mass of women were rushing to the water, the enemy had started for the first time to try to force the side gates that opened on to the river landing places: they had been beaten back, but if they succeeded in getting round to the river side of the fort even the retreat to the boats would be cut off. It was a new terror.

Whatever the reasons, an extraordinary scene now took place. As Drake was distractedly trying to quell the mob and issue orders to which no one paid the slightest attention, he looked down from the ramparts on the river side to see

Minchin, the fort's military commander, step into a small boat and row quickly off in the direction of the *Dodaldy*, some way downstream. Mr Mackett was with him, and the engineer John O'Hara as well. And the number of Europeans moving on to the dock with the same thought in mind was growing all the time.

Something in Drake must have snapped. He ran out of the fort and down to the landing stage, followed by a bewildered Captain Grant. Everyone assumed he was trying to stop Minchin deserting the fort, but his goal was another budgerow drawn up by the river bank, apparently ready and waiting. Grant was seen arguing and pleading with Drake, but then both men got into the boat and ordered the oarsman to row them, too, in the direction of the *Dodaldy*. There was utter confusion. Many people later claimed – probably quite honestly – that when they saw the governor and the military commander leaving, they thought the general order to retreat must have been given and they followed as best they could. About fifty Europeans deserted, but as Hill points out:

thus many gallant men who had gone on board with full leave from their superiors, who had no intention of deserting their comrades, and who had stayed on board only under the impression that a general retreat had been made, were involved in the shameful action of their commanders.

Mr Mackett, although he was worried about the serious condition of his wife Sarah after her miscarriage, actually tried to charter a boat to get back to the fort, and Captain Grant was probably caught on board the *Dodaldy*, not realizing the ship was going to set sail. Paul Pearkes, the chief accountant, wrote that 'Captain Minchin's going occasioned not the least concern to anyone, but it was with great difficulty we could persuade ourselves Captain Grant had left us.'

When the governor reached the *Dodaldy*, which was already packed with several times as many passengers as it was meant to carry, the ship began to move downriver almost straightaway. 'Upon Mr Drake's ship getting under sail,' wrote Tooke, one of those left in the fort, 'every ship followed his example, and in less than an hour's time not a boat was to be seen near the factory, nor a vessel in condition to move.'

For those left behind, who now clustered around the natural authority of Holwell, there was only one hope. The *Prince George*, the ship that had helped in the action at Perrin's redoubt, was still upstream, and messages were sent to Captain Hague, her commander, asking him to drop down and pick up all the rest of the defenders and take them to safety. It was a bright hope, but quickly extinguished: in full view of the fort and its increasingly desperate inhabitants, the ship's Dutch pilot misjudged a sandbank and ran the ship aground, where it stuck fast. It was so close, but it was useless. In the recriminations of the following year, it was claimed that the *Prince George* could easily have been refloated if Drake had agreed to send them up an extra anchor, when Captain Hague sent a message down to his ship asking for one. But he and Captain Young refused, saying they couldn't spare one: their passengers were too important to put at risk. The *Prince George* was left to its fate, and within a few days it had been looted and burnt by the nawab's forces.

It was an appallingly callous decision, not even to lend the spare anchor. The sufferings and deaths that came afterwards, Tooke wrote, were the responsibility of Drake and Young and Manningham as directly 'as if they had cut their throats'. Not only had they abandoned the garrison, 'but actually had it in their power to have saved every man's life afterwards' by helping to refloat the last remaining ship that could have taken them to safety and had decided not to.

Even so, why did Drake and Minchin not organize some-

one else to go back for the others, after the *Prince George* was
lost? There were several large ships that did not have the
excuse of being loaded to the gills with women and children;
each was armed with the same powerful guns that had devas-
tated the enemy at the start of the siege; they were so close
that they could see the fort. S. C. Hill rubs in the enormity
of this refusal by listing them, like a litany of indifference:
apart from the *Dodaldy*, there were the *Lively* and the *Diligence* (the tone of their names rings a note of irony), the *Fame*,
the *Ann*, the *Fortune*, the *London*, the *Neptune*, the *Calcutta*,
the *Hunter* and 'four or five other small vessels'. We can
picture the cluster of these magnificent sailing ships, bobbing
gently at anchor in the middle of the huge river. Small countries had been conquered with less. Yet there wasn't a ship
that could be persuaded to go back to the fort.

It is sometimes difficult to remember the status of these
ships. They were not part of the British navy, or even of the
Bombay Marine, an East India Company fleet of smaller ships
whose purpose was mainly to go after pirates. They were all
privately owned, by individuals or groups, for whom they
probably represented half a lifetime's wealth. Their captains
were autonomous, responsible only to their owners (in some
cases they were the owners), so they did not have to take
orders from Governor Drake, even if he had given any. Of
course they could have organized the rescue of the remaining
forces in the fort – these Indiamen were kitted out like
men-o'-war – if they had acted together. But each captain
had a great personal investment in the safety of his ship: the
rescue mission was considered 'too dangerous', and when
they spotted the signals flying from the fort they conveniently
decided that it was probably a trick by the enemy to get a
ship to return so that they could ambush it and decided to
ignore the flags. In fact, these were genuine distress signals
from the men left behind, who could not believe they had

been abandoned. Governor Drake later pleaded that he had cajoled, bribed and threatened ships to go back towards the fort, but it had been the native crews who had refused to sail. No one believed him. 'Never, perhaps,' says Orme in his best finger-wagging tone,

was such an opportunity of performing a heroic action so ignominiously neglected; for a single sloop with fifteen brave men on board might, in spite of all the efforts of the enemy, have come up, and anchoring under the Fort, have carried away all who suffered in the dungeon.

Inside Fort William, Holwell had taken control. Paul Pearkes, the Company accountant, claimed that he was the senior official – they still had time to quibble over niceties – but the assembled militia demanded that Holwell should be their leader. They had seen him fight. In all the controversy about the man, there was no doubt that he was good in a crisis and could provide the decisive leadership so lacking in the dithering Drake. Not everyone agreed that his motives were as selfless and heroic as he later made them sound in his endless reports to Leadenhall Street, though. Perhaps he had just, literally, missed the boat: several witnesses claim he was distraught when he found his own gone in the general rush at the waterside and couldn't find another. William Lindsay, a young Writer who had been allowed to leave on the *Dodaldy* because of a wounded leg, wrote that 'it was much against [Holwell's] inclination being there, two gentlemen having carried away the budgerow he had waiting for him. I mention this as I understand he made a merit in staying when he found he could not get off'.

This may have been true: the 45-year-old Holwell was a survivor rather than an altruist. But he did 'make a merit in staying'. Since he was trapped in the fort, he rose to the challenge, in his own way. Despite all the losses and desertions, there were still about 140 defenders, and Holwell set about organizing them for a last frenzy of resistance. It seems odd that he didn't immediately send messages of surrender to the nawab, but during this first day he was probably still hoping for a ship to come back for them.

He provided the men with the first hot meal they had had since the battle began, by the forceful but effective method of commandeering what he needed from the refugees – they were not all poor people, and some had managed to come into the fort with retinues of servants and family carrying cooking utensils. He carefully assessed the dwindling powder stocks that had caused so much trouble, and parcelled it out so that it might last the day. He was obviously a pragmatist: he even organized a reasonable supply of arak, so that the soldiers could have their tots of liquor without having to break into the stores to steal it and without becoming incapable.

That afternoon's fighting was some of the fiercest yet, but at first the men seemed to have new spirit. They even managed to set fire to some of the tall houses around the fort, and so destroy the enemy's vantage points (why had this not been done sooner?). But the death-toll was terrible that day, and by noon of the next there had been another twenty-five killed and seventy wounded, forty of them in a single action. With the *Prince George* broken-backed and ransacked, and the growing realization that no one was going to come and help them, the remaining soldiers lost their earlier morale, and it was impossible to keep order: the mercenaries were more drunken and crazy than ever, and that night a Dutch sergeant called Hedleburgh, whom some people had already suspected of being in touch with the enemy camp, arranged for a mass desertion of dozens of his fellow soldiers. There were only fourteen gunners left.

All this time, the figure who hovers over this story like a

turbulent spirit, Omichand, had been imprisoned in the Black Hole. One can imagine the state he was in, this man who had lived like the richest of princes, after spending several of the hottest days and nights of the year in a bare cell without a single amenity, in darkness and filth, in agonies of thirst and probably only with a little hard biscuit chucked through the grille when someone remembered to do so. Presumably, the unlucky Kissendas was in the Black Hole too, but he rather disappears from the record while the battle was on. A couple of days before, Drake had tried to persuade Omichand to write a letter arranging terms with the nawab, and he had haughtily refused, so furious was he at his treatment by the British.

It had been unwise of Drake to treat Omichand so roughly. Nothing had been proved against him, and if he had schemed and plotted before, he was just as capable of doing so now. Even as the battle was at its height, there were probably still informers in the fort – who could tell, among the hundreds of refugees? Any one of them could have sidled up to the grilles in the wall of the Black Hole in the darkness to receive Omichand's whispered instructions. Any silent figure who knew the way could have slipped out of the back of the fort, along the dark river bank under the walls and around into the enemy lines, which were hardly a hundred yards away. Nevertheless, Holwell, always the tactical politician, realized that his best hope was to negotiate a dignified submission. The nawab's forces had also suffered staggering losses, with many thousands of men dead (some reports say as many as 5,000), and it was obvious that Siraj would not be sorry to end the fighting. Holwell was experienced enough in the Indian codes of honour and dignity, however, to know that the capitulation had somehow to be made without displaying the true extent of the British weakness. Not exactly a complete surrender, otherwise the repercussions from the victor would be terribly cruel; more a termination of hostilities with honour intact. He had to talk to Omichand.

One of the strangest and most inconsistent bits of Holwell's later testimony, all the pages and pages of it, was his claim that he had never seen the Black Hole and so was not aware of its true size. Since he hadn't realized how small it was, he declared, he and the others had not put up a fight when they were later ordered into it. This seems more than unlikely, since it was in the corner of a parade ground where he had spent his working life for several years, and he was after all Calcutta's chief magistrate, so presumably he had had something to do with the prisons. Anyway, it was nothing but a walled-in section of a regular arcade – how much easier could it be, to estimate the size of something? And doubly so, since it is known that he went to see Omichand that day. But whether or not Holwell knew the inside of the place, Omichand certainly knew what it was like, intimately and bitterly. And Omichand, as everyone testified, never forgave a slight.

The story of what happened, from the point at which Drake and Minchin and the others deserted the fort, is like a perception test. The black lines are clearly drawn on the paper, but some people see two faces in profile, and other people see a candlestick. If you narrow your eyes, the profiles turn into a candlestick, or vice versa; with a little practice, you can refocus at will, to turn the incontrovertible facts into something else, something equally incontrovertible, and then back again.

Omichand agreed to write to the nawab. Or rather, to one of his closest advisers, Manik Chaund – the man who was to become the governor of Calcutta when it passed into the nawab's possession. Hardly, therefore, an impartial inter-mediary, but in this situation there was no such thing. The letter was supposed to broker an honourable peace between honourable opponents, and to ask for negotiations over what would happen next. But who knows what it really said? Letters had to be written by a scribe, who would be trusted to translate and put down accurately what was dictated to him; whether there was a scribe in the fort, or whether Omichand wrote it himself, is not recorded. But a letter was written and dispatched, and in the relief of the noonday calm Holwell fell asleep, sitting at the end of the long table in the cannon-blasted Council chamber, now more or less open to the sky, surrounded by rubble and filth, his head on the table.

In a remarkably short time, there came what appeared to be a reply to the letter. About 2 p.m., Holwell was called to the south-east bastion, where guards had spotted a lone officer of the nawab's army, grandly dressed in a turban of the royal indigo, walking towards the fort and making signals to the soldiers not to fire. The message he brought was that if the fighting stopped, negotiations for a settlement might begin. Holwell asked him to return with an assurance that the garrison would be treated properly, and a ceasefire was agreed. The flag of truce was hoisted, a deep quiet fell on the ruined streets outside the fort, a deep sense of relief inside it. Nothing stirred in the intense heat as everyone waited for the nawab's next move in the negotiations.

At four o'clock, the silence was shattered abruptly by commotion on all sides. In front of the fort, beside it, from every angle the nawab's soldiers were pouring out of the houses and buildings where they had been silently waiting, and crowding around the walls ready to attack. The British were utterly confused: in the ritual of warfare, they could not believe that the nawab would have broken his word and tricked them into a ceasefire. Siraj was cruel but he lived by a code of honour. Apparently Holwell stood up on top of walls, with several officers beside him, to see whether he could locate a messenger or intermediary; a shot rang out, but it missed

Holwell, and a young lieutenant named Baillie, who had been standing beside him, fell dead. The enemy soldiers rushed the walls with bamboo ladders, scaling them in their dozens, hacking at the defenders and swarming over the top and down into the fort. At the same time, news came that the gates to the river side had been opened from the inside, by the Dutch sergeant Hedleburgh, and dozens of the Dutch soldiers who had deserted the previous night, with a large number of the nawab's soldiers to swell their ranks, swarmed back into the fort, running wildly through the parade ground among the cowering and screaming refugees, attacking any English figure they could find, crashing their way into the rooms and offices with ransack and plunder on their minds. More and more poured in over the walls; more flooded in through the back gates. The last, awful stand against these invaders from every side was the bloodiest of all. Several of the young men who had fought through everything – Piccard and Blagg among them – were hacked to pieces by the swords and knives of the Indian soldiers, completely outnumbered, as the nawab's colours were already being hoisted on one of the fort's bastions on the river side.

Exactly what happened, and how the fighting stopped, is very confused in the survivors' accounts. It is almost impossible to imagine the chaos, the smoke, the carnage, as hundreds of Indian troops surging into the already crowded and ruined place were joined by the treacherous mercenaries who had been fighting for the British and therefore knew every cranny of the fort. The panic and terror among the refugees must have been intense; again hundreds made for the river, running wildly without any sense of what they were doing, and in their crazed rush to get away from the danger of being shot or hacked to death dozens drowned like lemmings.

The idea that anyone could have called a ceasefire in this situation is almost unbelievable, and how any of the British survived the frenzied mobs of invaders is almost incredible. Yet, according to Holwell, 'to the first jemmautdar [officer] who scaled the bastion I advanced and offered my pistols' – and that surrender, apparently, was enough to restore relative quiet, if not order. It implies a much higher level of discipline in the nawab's army than anyone gives it credit for: there were apparently no murderous reprisals, there was no spree of mutilation and killing. None of the refugees was deliberately harmed. The officer dealing with Holwell behaved very properly, and the nawab's soldiers could now get on with the interesting business of plundering everything in the fort unimpeded. They stripped the soldiers of anything of the slightest value – buttons, and the buckles on belts and shoes and musket-straps, as well as watches and rings – but apart from that they seemed hardly to know what to do with their prisoners.

In the Indian convention of the time, the taking of prisoners was not prescribed with the same formality as other processes of warfare. A few valuable figures might be taken away as ransom or trophy, and others might be carried off as slaves, but the rest would either be allowed to escape or get killed. Now what happened was that refugees from Black Town – any that remained – were simply shooed off, and must have wandered in a daze out of the fort and off back to the ruined remains of what had been their homes. Even a few of the British escaped at this point, although that is hardly the right word to describe simply walking out of the back gates while the Indian soldiers were too busy searching for loot to worry about their prisoners. In this way four or five Company men took the chance to make their way down the river bank under cover of the general confusion, and were picked up by the ships a few days later. Perhaps the nawab had even given orders that the prisoners should not be carefully watched; it would probably have suited him quite well if the British had evaporated away, as he may already have realized that he did not know what to do with them. In this surprisingly calm moment, Holwell and the other defenders who remained must have believed that they too would get reasonable treatment.

It seems very odd, this final storming of the fort. It is unlikely that Siraj would have broken his word about the truce, especially in only two hours. (Some commentators who knew him claimed that it was unthinkable not only because of the issue of his honour, which he took very seriously, but because he would not have been awake between two and four in the afternoon.) It is possible that two things were going on at the same time. Some people believed that Omichand's letter did not reach the nawab, or, if it did, it said something other than what was dictated, and that the first 'messenger' suggesting a ceasefire did not come from Siraj at all but was actually part of the plot by Hedleburgh and the Dutch deserters. They wanted to gain some time to organize their treacherous attack. It was loot, rather than conquest, that they had in mind, and their attack was motivated by the persistent rumours that there were huge stores of treasure somewhere in the fort. It may well have been orchestrated by Omichand. If this theory is right, then the nawab did not even know about the phoney truce, and his attack on the walls was a final push that just happened to coincide with the Dutch sergeant's plot.

Whether it was a single betrayal by the nawab, by the mercenaries or by Omichand, or whether it was a plot carefully planned between all three elements, we shall never know. Later, though, Holwell came under fierce criticism for the last, appalling debacle – why hadn't he simply sent a message of surrender to the nawab the day before? Many in the fort had pleaded with him to do so. But he was relentlessly ambitious, even in dire circumstances, and he had been very keen to have himself properly declared governor of the settlement and commander-in-chief – incredibly, this on-the-spot promotion, as well as the formal suspension of Drake and Minchin, was minuted in the Council records in formal copperplate, just as if there had not been a battle raging outside. Holwell probably thought he would be able to mount a heroic defence before the rescue, or capitulation if there had to be one, and do very well by taking the credit for it. But to try to hold out, even for twenty-four hours, had been crazy, not heroic, and it had cost hundreds of lives on all sides. Quite a number of men had been lost in the general pandemonium in the fort and on the river, several of the bravest young Company men had died awful deaths in the last, horrible, pointless massacre, and Holwell must have realized that he could have prevented all that. He was astute about how things would play back in London, and he knew he would have some explaining to do. It may have occurred to him, even then, that a good story about some of these deaths, a ripping tale of pathos and suffering and heroism, might be just what was needed.

The nawab entered Fort William from the river side. It was a narrow gate, but he might have wanted to emphasize the fact that the precious retreat was well and truly closed. Siraj liked to put on a show, and now in victory he stage-managed a splendid entrance after making a slow tour of the walls with his entourage. He sat on a magnificent open litter carried by huge dark slaves, elaborately dressed, and behind him rode a retinue of his senior commanders – St Jacques, Dulabh and others – on beautifully caparisoned horses. The procession was attended by ranks of uniformed guards as the litter was set down in the open space in front of Writer's Row. While further search parties scurried everywhere around the fort to bring the nawab news of what treasure was to be found, Siraj held a formal *durbah* in the traditional manner, sitting in his litter with his guards to attention around him, in the open, summoning one by one those he wished to speak to and addressing them so that everyone could hear.

There are some reports that the person he received first of all was Kissendas, who had been rather forgotten in the Black Hole all this time. This may have been because he was Siraj's kinsman, or because Siraj was hoping that Kissendas would tell him the whereabouts of the palace treasure with which the latter was rumoured to have absconded. Or perhaps (to satisfy the conspiracy theorists) it was proof that Kissendas had been used as a decoy right from the start. Omichand too had a royal audience, and the way in which he was treated left no one in any doubt about where his allegiances lay.

Then it was Holwell's turn. As the ragged, exhausted, middle-aged Englishman, bare-headed and in filthy tattered clothes stained with sweat and blood, stood before the magnificent and bejewelled prince, Cooke was one of the Company men within earshot. In his report on the conversation we get an evocative picture of the nawab's personality. Despite his victory, apparently, Siraj was peeved. Fed up. What Holwell got was a thorough ticking-off. The nawab complained about the battle and about all that had happened, and in a rather whining tone 'expressed much resentment at our presumption in defending the Fort against his army with so few men' and in causing him such terrible losses. And terrible they were: 'of the enemy,' Holwell reported later with some pride, 'we killed first and last, by their own confession, 5000 of their troops and 80 Jemadars and officers of consequence, exclusive of their wounded'. (With figures like these, it was unfair of Macaulay, a century later, to describe the resistance at Calcutta as 'feeble'.) Siraj was clearly as delighted with the town as a child with a new toy, however, and declared that the English were 'fools' to have made him destroy such a fine place. He was especially annoyed at the destruction of Government House, which he seemed to regard as his by right, but he had already installed himself very contentedly in one of the least badly damaged of the European mansions, the one that had belonged to Mr Wedderburn, a member of the Council. Siraj was curious to know why Holwell and the others had not run away with the governor. But most of all he 'seemed much disappointed and dissatisfied at the sum found in the treasury' – his men had only discovered money and goods to the value of about 50,000 rupees, or £6,000, far less than the fabled fortunes that were supposed to be locked up in Calcutta's treasury.

The whole question of Fort William's supposed treasure is another that rumbled on and on. Who saved the Company's deposits, if they did, and who took the Company's precious account books, without which no financial reckoning was possible? Some years later, at the end of their long and pretty much fruitless investigations, the East India Company comforted itself with the fact that so little, in the end, was left to be plundered by Siraj, because by lucky chance there was hardly anything in the fort's coffers at the time. But was that true? Rumour had it otherwise. Apart from anything else, all the Europeans who had taken refuge when the trouble started would have brought any valuables they could carry into the fort with them, for safe-keeping – they would never have left their portable wealth behind in empty houses. Almost everything they owned would have been in the form of cash or jewels, normally kept in their houses under lock and key, and under the guard of a small army of servants. So it seems only logical that there must have been large personal fortunes in jewels and precious objects as well as cash (none of which would have shown up anywhere in the Company's books) stored in the fort during the siege. If so, where had it all gone? Away with Manningham and Frankland, perhaps? Both these men were senior enough to have access to the treasury. And what about Drake – what did he take with him? Or, given that we can never underestimate the power of his network of spies and helpers, what might Omichand have organized during the confusion of the final battle, even from his prison cell?

The rumours about this immense treasure, and its fate, passed into melodrama in letters home from the French factories, where schadenfreude was the dominant emotion. 'The French,' as Hill puts it,

heard from native reports that Drake had embarked on the ships not only the Company's treasure, but the goods placed by the European and native inhabitants of Calcutta for safe custody in the Fort [and] upon this rumour [they] built up a romantic plot on the part of Drake, Manningham, and Frankland to ruin Calcutta simply with the object of enriching themselves. They refer to this as the 'Mystery of Iniquity' . . .

He admits that the conspiracy theorists could not quite account for the fact that, if there had been such a plot, the perpetrators might have shown a little more foresight about how to manage their getaway. But no one allowed logic like this to get in the way of a lurid story, and there were some who were ready to swear that Holwell had been part of the same plot, only that it had gone wrong on the confused night of the men's defection, and Holwell had found himself stranded without a boat. This idea of a bungled plan would explain a number of strange anomalies in the record, according to Iris MacFarlane, writing in the 1980s, and in particular it would explain why the ships refused to go back to help the fort at the very end: it was part of the plan that Calcutta should be destroyed by the enemy so that any losses would be attributed to plunder by the nawab and the dastardly Company men could make off with the real loot.

If there was a plot, and it went wrong, it was about to go very much further wrong now. The nawab's intense questions about the treasure finally came to an end, and Holwell tells us that 'on the conclusion he assured me on the word of a soldier that no harm should come to me, which he repeated more than once'. Dissatisfied though Siraj was, the royal train swept off at dusk, back to Mr Wedderburn's house or to their silken tents, leaving the British contingent sitting vacantly about in the filthy, deserted parade ground. It was in an appalling state: a bomb-site, literally, that had seen the lives and deaths of many hundreds of people living in the open over days of relentless heat. There would have been rubble and detritus, blood and excreta, vermin and waste, and pathetic corpses thrown or huddled into corners. There had been no way to bury bodies during the siege; the only thing to have done with the hundreds of dead would have been to chuck them in the river, or burn them on makeshift pyres, but after the vicious fighting of the day bodies and parts of bodies were still lying about, starting to putrefy in the heat and giving off an indescribable stench. They would have been glad of the vultures. It may have been partly because of the sheer state of the place, rather than just random destructive-ness, that had made Siraj's men set fire to several of the buildings within the fort.

The governor's house and parts of Writer's Row were burning brightly in the gathering darkness. The guards were as restless as their charges, not really knowing what to do. There were about 150 people, 'those who had borne arms, of all sorts and conditions, black, brown and white'. Most accounts agree that there was one woman among them. As Hill describes the bedraggled band of survivors, 'many of this shattered remnant were wounded; all were in a state of exhaustion. When it was dark they were directed to collect, all, without distinction, under the arched verandah, and to sit down quietly in one body. This they did, their backs being turned to the barracks and its prison, their faces looking west towards the parade ground', where there was a rank of guards with lighted torches.

The fires were blazing around them; they were afraid that they too were going to be burnt, or anyway suffocated by smoke. They were even more afraid when they saw the nawab's guard going from room to room around the fort with torches, but it turned out that they were only looking for a place to put the prisoners for the night. An application to the nawab's camp about what to do with the prisoners merely received the reply that they should be put wherever prisoners in the fort were usually put. In short, the nawab and his officers had gone off for the night and were not interested in the details. But one person who might have whispered a suggestion to the messenger could have been Omichand.

Holwell takes up the story of what happened when the officers of the guard finally decided to usher the group of prisoners into the barracks, the open arcade with its long sleeping platform against the wall:

In we went most readily, and were pleasing ourselves with the prospect of passing a comfortable night on the platform, little dreaming of the infernal apartment in reserve for us. For we were no sooner all within the barracks, than the guard . . . with their muskets presented . . . ordered us to go into the room at the southernmost end, commonly called the Black Hole prison; whilst others from the court of guards, with clubs and drawn scimitars, pressed upon those of us next to them. This stroke was so sudden, so unexpected, and the throng and pressure so great upon us there was no resisting it.

The crowd was shoved forward by the threatening soldiers and, although Holwell was at the front of the band of prisoners, 'like one agitated wave impelling another, we were obliged to give way and enter; the rest followed like a torrent, few amongst us, the soldiers excepted, having the least idea of the dimensions or nature of a place we had never seen; for if we had, we should at all events have rushed upon the guard, and been, as the lesser evil, by our own choice cut to pieces'.

These quotes are from the account of that hellish night written by Holwell some months later, in the form of a letter to a friend but fully intended for publication, on a homeward-bound ship. He has a dramatic turn of phrase, and in his description there are few hyperboles left untapped. After its publication in Britain the following year, its details were quickly known by heart to half the country, rehearsed, discussed, relayed and exaggerated, shuddered over. The 'letter' became the basis for a legend of horror that was to obsess the nation for many years to come.

It was about 8 p.m. on the night before the monsoon finally broke, the hottest and most humid of the whole year, a night when the temperature outside could hardly have dropped below 90 degrees, and when it is hard even to estimate, let alone imagine, the heat inside. There were fires burning all around the fort, and in this cell measuring 18 feet by about 14 feet there were, according to Holwell's account, 146 people, all struggling even to breathe the tiny amount of air that came in through the two small grilles set high in one wall of the cell.

He tells of hours and hours of misery and torture, agonies of thirst and exhaustion and crushing, as the dying slowly slithered to the floor in the pack of bodies and were trampled underfoot by the living, who were fighting for any extra inch of space. He describes those who died but couldn't even fall, because the crush was so bad that they were propped upright by the bodies around them, living and dead packed together without even room to turn around. He gives details of how some who were nearest the window grilles managed to squash some of their tricorn hats and pass them through the narrow bars to the gaolers, who would fill them with a few spoonfuls of water and pass them back, and the fighting that even the idea of water produced among these desperate people, 'every one giving way to the violence of passions' – 'words cannot paint to you the universal agitation and raving the sight of it threw us into'. It was such torture, these few spilled drops that only inflamed their thirst, and brought the guards grinning and jeering at the English fighting each other like animals to get to the water, that he stopped the hats travelling through the bars for the entertainment of the soldiers outside. 'How shall I give you a conception, my dear Sir,' he wrote,

of what I felt at the cries and ravings of those in the remoter parts of the prison, who could not entertain a probable hope of obtaining a drop, yet could not divert themselves of expectation . . . calling on me by the tender considerations of friendship and affection, and who knew they were really dear to me.

He describes how they pleaded with the guards outside, too, offering elaborate bribes of 1,000 rupees, 2,000, 5,000 or 10,000, more than a lifetime's pay for a soldier, but it was no use – the fear of what the nawab would do to them if they took pity on the prisoners must have outweighed this massive ransom. And how some of the prisoners even yelled insults at the guards hoping that they would fire into the cell and put an end to the agony.

He gives macabre images that linger in the mind: of how one man managed to get his hat above his face and fan himself for a little air, and then everyone tried to do the same, but that the heavy hats in such a space hit and cut the others in the face and how some even died with their arms pinned above their heads, holding their hats, as there was no room to lower them again, upright corpses in a ghastly parody of waving goodbye. Of how most of the men stripped off their clothes to be cooler, but that in some ways this was worse because the sweat streaming off the naked bodies made it harder for the weakest to remain standing, as 'now when a fainting man reached out for something to clutch, his fingers merely slithered off slippery skin'. Of how he tried drinking his own urine, but the rank smell only made him vomit, and then since he had decided to keep his shirt on he took to sucking one of the sleeves drenched with his own sweat, and managed to get a small amount of moisture that way; suddenly he felt something on his other arm, and realized that a huge Dutch soldier crammed beside him was sucking the other sleeve, like a baby feeding from its mother, without apology or even comment. Young Henry Lushington started to do the same; their noses and mouths sometimes bumping in a parody of kissing.

Once someone had dropped to the floor, there was little hope of survival. Even if the people above had wanted to avoid crushing those below, it would have been impossible, as they all blundered and staggered in the blackness, all trying to push their way towards the minute window embrasures, slithering on urine and blood and vomit, taking advantage in their desperation of any gap left by a fallen body, clambering over two or three or more piled up as the rapid deaths left more room for the living. Some were severely wounded anyway, from the days of battle and the fierce fighting that morning; they were all probably in a chronic state of dehydration when they were imprisoned, since water had been scarce for the days of the siege: he reports that perhaps fifty people died in the first hour or so, the others more slowly throughout the night.

His account is vividly peopled by the figures we know:

the Reverend Bellamy and his son John, a Writer who had fought all the way through the siege, hand in hand with each other as they both slipped into semi-delirium, then away altogether into death; the awful adjutant Clayton, for whom no one had ever had a good word, dead like an animal, face upwards on the growing heap of bodies; Leach, the Company carpenter, dead on his feet and held upright by the squash of men around him; Mary Carey, who had managed to find a place on the narrow platform that ran across the back of the cell, cradling her husband Peter in her arms as he slowly but relentlessly lost the battle for life and air, unable to endure any more.

During the night Holwell too at one point decides he can bear no more, and leaves the window nook that was enabling him to breathe and crosses the room, wading knee deep in bodies, and eventually passes out, on the verge of death until some of the younger and stronger men, Lushington, Cooke, Mills, found him already submerged under other bodies and managed to pull him free and revive him.

Throughout Holwell's account the reader is torn between horror and pity, and sheer disbelief. The first detail that strikes us as odd is about the door. Holwell makes a point of telling us that it opened inwards, so whatever they did they couldn't force it – but then how, with so many people crowding into the room, did it get shut in the first place? Such practical details have provoked questions to which there is apparently no good answer. How did Holwell manage to recognize people and see what they were doing, and give graphic descriptions of their condition, even the expression on their faces and the moment of their death, especially if they were at the back of the room? It would have been blacker than pitch – yet at several points in his account he seems to have been able to take out his watch (how was it not looted from him earlier?) and read the time. And so on. There is a plethora of petty information that seems fantastical and even preposterous the more we look at it. But this account was written for emotional impact, many months later, and the fact that the details may have been exaggerated or actually invented does not necessarily invalidate the truth of the whole thing.

It does, however, make us wonder why Holwell went to such trouble to embroider a description that turned what was undoubtedly a horrifying event into a vivid, Dantesque vision of hell. Perhaps because he was setting a scene in which any number of people could have met their deaths, and any precise count or identification of those who died was almost impossible. Of the victims, only a dozen or so are reliably identified; all we know about many others is that they disappeared at some point, perhaps during that Sunday night, perhaps before it. Several experiments have been done, in an effort to discredit Holwell's story, and it is clear that 146 adults simply cannot fit into a space the size of the Black Hole, unless they are piled on top of each other. But the numbers game is not really the most important thing.

Other accounts, principally those of Cooke and Mills, became significant pieces of evidence in the Company's investigations later. They bear Holwell out, by and large, although their prose is much less purple. And once we have read one description of the night, it's no surprise to find that their lists of casualties and survivors do not exactly tally. It might be more suspicious if they did.

All through the terrible night, the prisoners had been pleading with the guards to send a message to the nawab. They did not believe he had meant them to suffer in this way. So although the cruelty was often laid to his account as a deliberate atrocity by later generations, the victims themselves thought it must have been a mistake. Or, if it were instigated by anyone, it was more likely to have been Omichand, who could have whispered in the nawab's ear that there was a convenient place in which to keep his captives safe overnight, knowing that he was far too grand to concern himself with such details as the dimensions of prison cells. In their desperate situation, the captives knew they had one trump card, which is that the nawab would not want Holwell to die in the night – he was still convinced that the settlement's chief could be made to tell him where precious treasures were hidden.

But no guard could be induced to have the nawab disturbed: it was more than their life was worth. Only towards dawn, at about 5 a.m., did one of Siraj's senior officers hear the first rumours of what had been going on all night at the fort, and he went to see whether Holwell was still breathing. He conveyed such a picture of horror to Siraj that the orders were immediately given to open the cell and let the prisoners out.

Now, at the very end, Holwell does give us a detail that rings true. When the frightened guard at long last unlocked the door, in the fresh morning air, it still couldn't be opened. The weight of the bodies piled up against it on the inside held it fast, even against the shoving of strong soldiers. There was nothing for it but for the few inside who were still alive and capable of standing to move the corpses, one by one, dragging them up on to the higher piles of the dead further inside the cell that had become a stinking charnel house. They were so weak that this gruesome task took them another, endless, twenty minutes. Finally, at 6.30 a.m., almost eleven hours after they had been crammed in to the hell-hole of the night, twenty-two men and one woman emerged, 'the ghastliest forms that were ever seen alive, from this scene of horror'.

9. Aftermath

A literal translation of a letter sent to Mr George Piggott, Governor of Madras, by Surajud Dowlett, nabob of Muxadabad, after the taking of Calcutta, July 1756:

To the Principal or Head of all Merchants, Mr Piggott, who has always in remembrance the favour of God – It never entered into my heart or thoughts to deprive the English company of trading in Bengal, but Mr Roger Drake, your gomastah, is a very bad man, and gave harbour and protection to those that had accounts with the King. I did everything in my power to make him sensible that he was wrong, but he, without shame, persisted in his resolution. Those who come here for the service of the Company, why do they act in this manner? He, Mr Roger Drake, being a very bad man and without shame, is punished accordingly, and is gone from the subaship. Mr Watts, being a good man and without fault, we have despatched to you, who we esteem to be greatly in the Company's favour, for which reason we have wrote you the news of this bad man. Year the third of the King's reign and the first of the Shawant Moon, [signed] Seir Raja Dowlett.

The utter illogic of this letter shows the struggle historians have had to make sense of the web of motives and intrigues surrounding the loss of Calcutta. When Siraj says that it 'never entered into [his] heart or thoughts to deprive the English Company of trading in Bengal', is he being mendacious? By this time, the smaller British factories up-country had been forced to surrender as well: at Dacca the nawab's plunderers had found much more satisfactory reserves of money and silver. Or was Siraj already regretting his uneasy victory over a ruined town and the consequent loss of tax revenues? Or had he really convinced himself that it was nothing but hatred of Drake, the 'very bad man', that caused all the trouble? His return to the sore subject of 'those that had accounts with the King' – i.e. Kissendas – implies that his cousin had played no part in any plot, yet when the battle was over Kissendas seemed not only to be restored to the royal favour but treated as a hero of the hour. And Siraj's obvious attempt to have Watts installed in the 'subaship' – i.e. governorship – in Drake's place shows how clumsy a politician he was.

Perhaps what we have to infer from Siraj's contradictions is that he was (as several people have argued) a man who had very little conception of the world beyond his own horizons, the horizons of Bengal. Britain, Europe, the extent of its population and degree of its sophistication were things about which he neither knew nor cared. He seemed to think that its whole population was about 12,000 – M. Jean Law, the Chief of the French settlement at Murshidabad, wrote that Siraj had claimed he could control Europeans with 'a pair of slippers' because there were so few of them. He had only seen a few hundred Europeans, spread out over the whole of Bengal, so perhaps he simply contrasted this with his own teeming population and arrived at a wild misestimation of what Europe was. Thus he had no idea of what was to come his way, or of the extent to which he had done exactly what his grandfather Alivardi had warned him against – disturbing the nest of the honeybees.

For the moment, however, Siraj had his triumph. What he did next also bears out the suspicion that he could be hasty in his reactions. Omichand and Kissendas were already recovering from their own Black Hole ordeal in the nawab's camp, restored to their perfumed silks and waited on hand and foot by a swarm of retainers, when the twenty-three 'ghastly forms' staggered out of the same prison into the morning cool. The two powerful Indians would have lost no time in murmuring into the victor's ear, telling him to keep looking for the fabulous riches he had expected to find in the fort, and to persist in demanding to know their hiding-place. Even though they themselves may have had copious amounts of the British valuables already safely stashed away, this would have been sweet revenge.

Siraj had already renamed his trophy town Ali-nagore (the City of Ali) and ordered the building of a mosque in one corner of the ruined fort, but he was determined that he should also have its riches. The persistent lure of treasure was the only reason why he would have turned up in person to see a few bedraggled prisoners semi-conscious on the parade ground that June morning. They had half-crawled out of the Black Hole, the small band of survivors, and lay gasping for air and water on the open ground as the Indian soldiers were already beginning to haul the reeking corpses out of the cell behind them, roughly piling them high on to open carts and driving them out of the fort to the closest and easiest place where they could be disposed of – only 50 yards from the gates, in the piece of land that, just a week earlier, had been The Park, Calcutta's pretension to an elegant meeting place for evening drives and walks. There the soldiers tipped the dead bodies into the defensive ditch that had been roughly hacked across the open ground in the last few days before the siege began, and covered them equally roughly. It was done as quickly as possible, this revolting task, to get rid of the stench and the threat of disease and to beat off the circling vultures before the day got any hotter. There was no attempt even to count the bodies, let alone make any record of who they were. And there is a coda to the poignant horrors of the night in one or two of the survivors' testimonies, because they mention almost in passing that some of those who did not make it out of the cell showed signs of life, and could probably have been revived with a little attention: these people were probably buried alive.

Every one of the survivors of the Black Hole came out in a terrible rash of boils. These huge and painful lesions full of pus must have been their bodies' post-traumatic reaction, a consequence of extreme dehydration; as they put it at the time, 'for excess of sweating'. And the boils were only one of the sufferings to be endured in the next few days. Whether anyone gave the survivors water or food is not recorded, but for Holwell, and several others, the ordeal was not over.

The nawab sent for Holwell, and seeing that he was unable to stand upright or speak, ordered that something be brought for him to sit on. It was apparently 'a large folio volume', or several: this curious detail about the half-fainting Holwell propped by the guards on a pile of books in front of the angry nawab is one that has echoed down the centuries. Siraj questioned Holwell again about the money and issued horrible threats about what would happen to him if he didn't reveal what he knew. But Holwell genuinely knew nothing and may have been almost past caring. Something in his attitude must have convinced the nawab, or perhaps he just got bored; capriciously, he suddenly wanted to get rid of his captives and announced that every European should 'quit the place before sunset under the penalty of cutting off their nose and ears'. Equally capriciously, he decided not to release Holwell, however, and chose apparently at random three others to stay behind: a young ensign called Walcot and two Company men called Court and Burdett. These four were handed over as prisoners to one of Siraj's generals, Mir Mudin, to see whether he could get any information out of them.

Henry Lushington, still only eighteen years old, was one of the survivors who somehow found his way out of the ruins of Calcutta, together with Cooke and Mills, two sailors called

Dickson and Moran, and several others. They eventually managed to reach the other refugees at Fulta. But at this point we again lose sight of Mary Carey. Perhaps she went back to Black Town, to find some remnants of family or friends; perhaps it is simply because we don't know what happened to her next that the harem rumour gained such currency – spurred on by Holwell's enigmatic comment that she was 'too young and handsome' to be released. Even at a time when all Europe seemed ready to assume that the Muslims were intent on carrying off white women at every possible opportunity, and such legends were common currency, this was a remarkably persistent rumour. The Frenchman Jean Law published a memoir less than ten years later that claimed that 'a woman was amongst [the survivors], also M. Holwell, and four or five officers and Company's servants. The woman was placed in the Nawab's harem. She was, I believe, the wife of one of the Ganges pilots.' Asiaticus, the pseudonym of a journalist called John Hawkesworth, tells a version of the story even more lavishly about thirty years later:

An English lady who saw her husband perish at her feet survived that miserable catastrophe, and the tyrant was so captivated with her beauty that he promoted her to the honour of his bed, and she remained seven years in his seraglio, when she was released at the request of Governor Vansittart, and is now alive at Calcutta.

But as Busteed points out, the bit about seven years is a stumbling block: 'it is unfortunate for this writer's gossip,' he remarks, 'that "the tyrant" himself only survived the catastrophe for one year'.

Robert Orme, who was on the spot, has a variation on the theme which suggests that Mary was taken to Mir Jaffir's harem; almost a century later, Macaulay reverts to the original version, that has Mary in the clutches of Siraj.

This is the Chinese-whispers school of history. Busteed tells us that he had a letter from a former Calcutta resident, a Mrs Beveridge, who had a copy of Holwell's 'Tracts' that contained some notes in the back. The first was written by Thomas Boileau about his visit to the 58-year-old Mary Carey, on 13 August 1799, 'between the hours of ten and eleven o'clock, by appointment, at her house in Calcutta, situate in an angle at the head of the Portuguese Church Street'. This was the interview in which she endorsed Holwell's description of events that night, and mentioned her mother and sister, who had died in the Black Hole.

The second note records, quite simply, that 'Mrs Carey died Saturday, March 28th, 1801.'

The third, in different handwriting, notes that 'Mrs Carey was made the subject of some very pleasing Latin verses by Dr Bishop, Headmaster of Merchant Taylor's School (where Clive was educated)'. And it gives the translation of the highly sentimental and fanciful verses:

When, by the command of an Eastern tyrant, a captive band suffered, alas! a cruel fate in the Fort at Calcutta, and on all sides strong men fell, maddened by thirst and dying with heat, a woman outlived the weakness and the horror, a woman endured all the turns of such varied misery. She saw her husband breathe his last at her feet, and was about to yield herself to a like death, when lo! the waters leap from her eyes as from springs, and bedew her lips with moisture. Grief gives her life. She cannot die of thirst, to whom fidelity itself thus gives tears for drink.

With this sort of sentimentalized nonsense, Mary passed into myth. Whether she was the beautiful teenage widow snatched away into the tyrant's harem, like the heroine of a gothic novel, or the grieving statue fed by her own tears, like the subject of a Greek myth, there was no reality to her. They couldn't grasp her; they couldn't really find her. And we can't find her either, the young woman who 'endured all the turns of such varied misery', any more than these earlier commentators could. All we know is that she somehow found her Mr Weston, or perhaps Captain Weston, not too long afterwards, and married him, and had two or three children – although where those children were on her burial in 1801, which is recorded in the cathedral register as a lonely event attended only by a single priest, we do not know. But their descendants were still around in Calcutta in about 1905. At that point, these good people put up a screen of respectability between themselves and the historical record, and Busteed solemnly says that he was informed by 'a European gentleman of the highest respectability and intelligence (since dead)' that Mary's relatives were 'unwilling, as many retiring people are, to have any direct reference made to them by name in print'.

This is the brick-wall school of history. Even though Busteed can't resist a tease – 'in deference to [the family's] feeling,' he continues, 'I am not able to mention a good deal of what the gentleman I allude to told me' – here we have a historian who tells us that he knows things about his subject (though he can't tell us what) on the authority of someone (though he can't tell us who) who knew what he knew from the descendants of the subject (but he can't tell us who they were either). There's just one thing he can tell us, and does, and it is that 'Mrs Carey was not carried off by the Moors'. The whole harem story was an invention.

This long-running shaggy-dog story about Mary and the harem probably all stemmed from Holwell's more or less casual remark – when he said that Mary was too young and handsome to be given her liberty immediately, perhaps he only meant that the guards detained her for a while, and perhaps even abused or insulted or mistreated her, before letting her go. He wasn't interested in following the fate of any other survivors and wasn't in any case in a position to know what happened to them, because he was caught up in his own horrors.

The next, awful days are recorded by Holwell in the letter in which he describes the Black Hole – in fact, at least half of it is taken up with his own experiences after the release from the cell. They make harrowing reading, and we can understand why he wanted to record them, but it's hard to escape the persistent note of self-justification that runs through it all.

The four prisoners were shoved on to an open cart – no doubt one of the carts that had just been used to dispose of the stinking corpses – and Mir Mudin had them transported to (where else?) Omichand's garden. No doubt Mir Mudin kept them there in the remains of the nawab's departing camp while he decided what to do with them; despite their condition, and the agonizing state of their skin, they were put in heavy chains, wrists and ankles. He decided to send them to Murshidabad. The journey by river on a small leaky open boat took a fortnight, and the four men lay chained on rough bamboo planking, often half immersed in water, day and night, sometimes in danger of drowning. The monsoon had broken; the rain pelted down mercilessly on their exposed bodies. They were given a very little rice and expected to drink from the river, however murky and polluted it was – although Holwell's medical background was enough to make him comment that this restricted diet may have saved their lives.

The torture of this slow journey is vividly described in Holwell's account. He had a way with words, and he even pre-empted his readers' disbelief when he wrote: 'There are some scenes in real life so full of misery and horror that the boldest imagination would not dare to feign them for fear of shocking credibility.' And here were the scenes. How they could hardly turn over, chained together on rough bamboo planks for hours on end; how they could hardly walk, when they were made to, because of the chafing of the irons on their boil-encrusted legs and ankles; their sickness and fever and misery. How the other Europeans – Dutch and French – tried to help them and offer clothes and food as they passed by the various settlements, but with a kindness that stopped short of actually insisting on their release, for fear of annoying the nawab and losing their own trading privileges. And how the condition they were in by the time they reached Murshidabad, and were paraded through the streets in their chains to the jeering of the crowds before being chucked into the common gaol for several days, would have evoked concern in even the 'most brutal'. When they were brought before the nawab again, Holwell was convinced that 'if [Siraj] is capable of pity or contrition, his heart felt it then. I think it appeared in spight of him, in his countenance.'

Pity, or contrition – or perhaps just a sudden and whimsical decision that after all Holwell didn't know anything about any treasure? Whatever the reason, Siraj abruptly ordered that the prisoners should be set free. It was 17 July, almost a whole month after the Black Hole ordeal, weeks of deprivation and pain for Holwell and his fellow captives. Yet, extraordinarily, Holwell was still capable of keeping his eye on the political situation, and on the need to communicate with London as quickly as possible, for it was from the Dutch settlement at Murshidabad on that day that he wrote the first of the hugely long and detailed letters about the loss of Calcutta and all that had happened. If his ordeals of the previous weeks had been as he described, it is almost impossible that he would have been able to write at all, let alone at such length and so coherently.

The Dutch at Murshidabad were kind; the Dutch far downriver at Fulta were even kinder. But Fulta, where the four British survivors now made their way, was severely overcrowded. Just as they landed and finally got to safety, Ensign Walcot died. But the other three went on to join the rest of the sad band that had been camped there for a month already, in the middle of the monsoon, on a bare bend of the river. There were no houses or any other shelter for the four or five hundred refugees who had landed there after the fall of Calcutta: far too many to be taken into the small Dutch settlement. Several of the large ships that had left the besieged Fort William were now anchored in the Hooghly near Fulta, and when Holwell and the others reached the place on 7 August they found the refugees, as Orme reported, 'obliged to sleep on board the vessels, which were so crowded that all lay promiscuously on the decks, without shelter from the rains of the season'.

They had lost everything. They did not even have a change of clothes. They were unprotected from the pouring rain. A 'malignant fever' infected all the ships; people were dying. British people who had been used to 'the gentle ease of India' – servants, wealth, respect, position – were living like the poorest street-people of the mighty cities they were helping to found. But, to go back to Orme, 'instead of alleviating their distresses by that spirit of mutual good will which is supposed to prevail amongst companions in misery', they were playing politics. The ineffable Drake had declared himself governor, once again, of the assembled group, and had taken himself off to the furthest ship, the *Fort William*, where he insisted on being treated with all the pomp attendant to his rank. All the rest were either engaged in fabricating excuses for themselves, because of their desertion of Fort William, or in trying to nail the ones who had. Everyone saw their misfortune as something they might profit from – if they got out alive.

In this extraordinary situation, among refugees who had

nothing, whose children were dying of fever and who had to sleep piled up in the open, in 'country so inundated that one cannot even erect a straw hut', there was still the urge to maintain formality and protocol. Drake re-established the Council, and under all the circumstances this note from him to Holwell, once the former magistrate had arrived in Fulta, is almost surreal:

Sir – Had not our boat been so extremely leaky, I proposed doing myself the pleasure of waiting on you this morning. We have concluded to meet on shore, on Mondays, Wednesdays and Fridays. It will be an infinite satisfaction that you will be pleased to join us, particularly to me who esteem your advice, and who am, very truly,

Your, &c, Roger Drake, Junior.

Between the ships memos went back and forth, as they quarrelled about precedence and bills for damage, about supplies and provisions, about who should be in what role, and who should communicate with the wider world. This last was a contentious issue, because so many of the senior figures were in disgrace.

'Honourable sir:' thundered a letter of protest to Drake from the junior officers,

Understanding that Charles Manningham, Esq., intends going to Madras in order to represent the unfortunate loss of Calcutta and the situation of the remaining part of the Colony; as that gentleman and Mr Frankland left the place before any retreat was agreed to and afterwards refused joining your Councils when sent for, contrary to both their duty and honour, we are of the opinion that either of those gentlemen are most unfit to represent transactions, which (as they absented themselves) they must know very little of, and therefore request that neither they nor any member of the Council may be permitted to abandon the remains of the Colony and the Company's effects scattered throughout the country.

Drake's reply was an emotional challenge to his accusers, in a letter nailed to the mast of every ship at anchor in the Hooghly, demanding that they 'acquaint me publickly of the censure that in their judgement I merit' – the squabbles went on and on. William Tooke was one junior trader who dared to take up Drake's challenge, and wrote a list of all his superior's failings: in his long letter he left us one of the clearest and finest accounts of the story. It is just one of several. Apart from professional self-preservation, there was good reason why so many individuals wrote up their versions of events.

Despite the controversial mission to Madras by the treacherous Manningham, no single, formal account of all that had happened was ever sent to London. This was for the simple reason that the surviving members of Council could not agree on what to say, and no one could devise a version to which they would all put their signatures. Accusations and counter-claims flew around the refugee camp as they remained stranded on their river bank, month after month. The Council wrote to Leadenhall Street from Fulta on 17 September, promising a proper and definitive account, but it never materialized, and finally in a letter of the following January they were forced to say that they 'left the Directors to draw their own conclusions from the several private and official letters already transmitted'.

In other words, everyone had had their say. All they could do was to wait for the interminable sea-journeys to be over, for their news to reach the outside world, for rescue. Because of the huge time-lag, the urgent cries for help they had sent off to Madras early in June, when Kassimbazar fell to the nawab's army, were only now getting a practical response in the form of ships and troops from Madras – but they too had their problems and the first arrived at Fulta with disease on board, reporting the loss of thirty-two out of 150 men on the way.

Eventually, after an unusually long wait, the shattering news of Calcutta's loss reached Europe. 'All London is in a consternation!' proclaimed the *Courrier d'Avignon* on 27 May of the following year, 1757. It was an imaginative headline, but all London was definitely not in a consternation at that point: all London was still in blissful ignorance of any turbulence in Bengal. It was not until several days later, on 2 June, that the *London Chronicle* published a short report, as picked up from Paris, and on 4 June the troubling news was confirmed by letters that arrived on the *Portfield*, the *Edgecote* and the *Chesterfield*, all of which had reached port together on the Irish coast on 28 and 29 May, about a week after the news had got to Paris.

If the news had reached the French first, it may have been nothing but an accident of the sailing ships and their variable journeys. It may, however, have had something to do with the delays of the British in sending off their reports: even when they stopped fighting among themselves about who should take the news to Madras, they agreed that no message should be sent to London until they could simultaneously send news of a rescue mission for the lost settlement. They knew what kind of a blow it would be in Leadenhall Street: the damage done to the Company was almost impossible to estimate, but was probably somewhere around 9.5 million rupees; once Robert Clive reached Bengal, he wrote back to London that he reckoned the private losses of the British must amount to £2 million. Furthermore, trade in the whole area was ruined, because the powerful Indian merchants were wary of dealings with the Europeans. Apart from the loss of life and the loss of reputation and dignity, it was a mighty amount of money to lose, and the directors had to act as fast as they could to quell the panic among shareholders. By this time there were few large businesses that did not depend in some way on the ships from the east – to lose the biggest and most important trading post in Bengal was something felt by many thousands.

For once, the vagueness of sailing times had worked well in the Company's favour. The ships bringing the bad news had taken a very long time to reach Europe, but it was only a few more weeks until the *Syren* arrived, having made the journey from Calcutta in only five months, with the information that the forces from Madras led by Robert Clive, assisted by Admiral Watson and his warships, had ousted the nawab and retaken possession of Fort William in February 1757. Siraj had lorded it over Ali-nagore for just seven months. Also on board the *Syren* was Holwell, with the long letter he had written on the way home.

Once the Court of Directors had digested the avalanche of letters that now descended on them from Bengal, arriving by every available ship with contradictory versions of events, accusations and counter-accusations, haughty self-exculpation and low spite, they launched an inquiry that came up with almost nothing. So many had died, and already so much time had passed; other dramatic events in Bengal were already superseding the impact of Calcutta's loss. All that interested the Company was to restore its fortunes and its trading potential; they were not in the business of conducting courts martial. It was all over surprisingly quickly, and with surprisingly few repercussions. In the whole shabby story, the only person to be dismissed by the Company was Captain Minchin, the deserting military commander. The directors summoned him back to London, but, since they had already sacked him, he chose to disobey their orders to leave and remained in Calcutta instead; he died there less than two years later.

The desertion of the governor and senior Council members was an embarrassment, but the ever-pragmatic Company decided that it was not a sacking offence. Thus Drake, Manningham and Frankland all survived in the Company's service, although the governor was demoted to the rank of senior merchant, a grade below a Council member. He retired to England after another few years, and died there at the age of forty-three. The other two, Manningham and Frankland, the joint owners of the *Dodaldy* and the cause of so much dissent, were not only reinstated but quite soon promoted.

Several others among the older men went on to good careers in the Company, especially Cooke, whose testimony of the Black Hole events is one of the most important corroborations of Holwell's account. Mackett, too, whose wife Anne had suffered a miscarriage during the siege, became a prosperous senior merchant. But the hardships of the stay at Fulta caused almost as many fatalities as the fighting and the imprisonment, because the refugees' overcrowded ships were so vulnerable to disease. Lady Russell died there, a few months after the loss of Calcutta, and so did Dorothy Bellamy, the wife of the bibulous Reverend who had died in the Black Hole together with one of their sons. Another son had been killed in the defence of the fort. Sarah Mapletoft, who had given birth to a baby daughter while the battle was raging, survived the ordeals at Fulta with her three small children, but her vicar husband caught the fever and died.

Some of the younger men found themselves caught up in violent action again soon afterwards, with tragic results. William Tooke, whose long report written at Fulta gives us such a vivid picture, was among Clive's forces at the battle to capture Chandernagore the next year: as Clive's journal records, he 'received a shot through his body, of which he soon died'. Henry Lushington, the eighteen-year-old who had fought all the way through the siege and survived the Black Hole, was killed in an uprising when he was twenty-five.

These were short and highly eventful lives of young men whose deaths make poignant reading. Others in this story lived on, sometimes equally eventfully. Frances Watts, the then pregnant wife of William Watts, the factor at Kassimbazar who was captured by the nawab's forces, had a special place in the fast-living Calcutta that rose from the ashes after the siege. She had been born in India, the daughter of Edward Croke, a governor of Madras. Before the good Mr Watts she had already buried two husbands. One was called Parry Templar, whom she seems to have married at thirteen, and with whom she had two children who both died; the next was James Altham, who succumbed to smallpox within days of their marriage. With William Watts she had four children, of whom two survived (her daughter Sophia married the Earl of Liverpool and was the mother of a British Prime Minister), but when Watts in his turn died she got married for the fourth time, still only in her twenties, to the Reverend Johnson of Calcutta. Through these vicissitudes she seems to have acquired a large fortune, and in the later eighteenth century her grand style of living became a byword for the luxurious life in the east. Begum Johnson, as she was always known, was the grande dame of Calcutta society, celebrated for her whist-parties, her hookah pipes and her snuff, for her magnificent house, elaborate dress and the brilliantly liveried servants who carried her everywhere in a decorated palan-quin. She has a starring role in William Hickey's *Memoirs*, and when Eliza Fay published her *Original Letters from India* in 1779, Begum Johnson's fame spread further. The Reverend Johnson retired to England, probably exhausted, but the Begum stayed on and died in 1812 at the age of eighty-seven, Calcutta's oldest resident.

Captain James Mills, another important chronicler of the

events of 1756, lived even longer than Begum Johnson, and died in London in 1811 at eighty-nine. For some years he had subsisted on only a small pension from the Company arranged for him by friends, as his fortune was long gone: on leave in England after the Black Hole, he had married a celebrity of the English stage, a 'bewitching' Mrs Vincent, who 'loved him for the dangers he had passed'. He brought her back to Calcutta, where their style of life probably rather exceeded his income.

When Captain Mills died, an obituary in *The Gentleman's Magazine* claimed that he was not in fact the last survivor. John Burdett, a young volunteer from among the Company's writers, had fought through the siege, emerged alive from the Black Hole and was one of the three others taken as prisoner with Holwell in chains to Murshidabad. He survived all this, and the disease-ridden months at Fulta too; although we seem to have no record of when he actually did die, in 1811 he was still alive and living in Totton, near Southampton. But if he, like many of the Writers, had been in his teens at the time of the attack by Siraj, he would have been about seventy-three when the magazine article was written. If it was true, he would have been the last person still alive who had experienced the dramatic events of fifty-five years before.

Holwell himself lived to a fine age. When he sailed back to London on the *Syren* in 1757, his health was very poor and he was already in his mid-forties. But he seemed to have remarkable powers of recovery from all that he'd been through, and he was back in Calcutta by the end of the following year. As ever with Holwell, there was some muddle about his exact appointment: at first, it appeared that the grateful directors in London had nominated him as successor to Robert Clive, who was by then the governor of Bengal. But some seemed to prefer the infamous Manningham for the job, others mistrusted Holwell, and he was relegated to ninth in Council. When he got to Calcutta, however, deaths and departures of more senior figures had already moved him up the hierarchy, and by 1759 he was the second most senior official. So when in February of 1760 Clive left for a spell in Europe, Holwell automatically stepped up to become acting governor.

It was the summit of his ambition, and he revelled in it: to the end of his life he liked to be known as 'Governor' Holwell. Sadly for him, it was short-lived, and after only a few months came the news that the permanent appointment had gone to someone else. Busteed records a revealing snippet from a gossipy letter written from Calcutta to the former Governor Drake: 'as soon as [Holwell] heard of Mr Vansittart's appointment, he seemed greatly shocked, but with his usual gaiety, and taking a pinch of snuff, said he was glad of it, for the fatigue of the chair was too much for him . . .'

After this, Holwell's career with the Company came to an ignominious end. Imputations of financial shenanigans never seemed far from Holwell, and he had powerful enemies in Leadenhall Street. Already reproachful letters were going back and forth to London; moreover, Clive had a great aversion to Holwell, whom he never trusted, and the two men seem to have got on unusually badly. From the directors' side, there were acrimonious comments about the management of the place. A letter from the Calcutta Council to the directors just a month before Clive left, in December 1759, complains strongly about their tone: 'Permit us to say that the diction of your letter is most unworthy [of] yourselves and us, in whatever relation considered, either as master to servants or as gentlemen to gentlemen . . .'

Whatever had happened to merit the ticking-off from Leadenhall Street, it was obviously some financial irregularity. The signatories, among them Holwell, Manningham, Frankland and Mackett, were highly indignant to 'have been treated in such language and sentiments as nothing but the most glaring and premeditated fraud could warrant', and hurt that the 'breath of scandal' could 'blow away in one hour the merits of many years service'.

This was one of those letters that became a victim of the tides, and took an unusually long time to reach home; the reply took even longer. It was more than a year before the directors' furious response arrived in Calcutta:

We do positively order and direct that immediately upon the receipt of this letter, all those persons still remaining in the Company's service who signed the said letter of the December 29, viz. Messrs J. Holwell, etc, be dismissed from the Company's service . . .

The disgraced men were not to stay in India, the directors ordered in their Big Brother mode, but were to sail on the first available ship. It was too late, in Holwell's case: he had already gone. He went voluntarily in September of 1760, after writing bitterly to Governor Vansittart that:

the many unmerited, and consequently unjust remarks of resentment that I have lately received from the present Court of Directors, will not suffer me longer to hold a service, in the course of which my steady and unwearied zeal for the honour and interest of the Company might have expected a more equitable return.

So the hero of the Black Hole left Calcutta, in something close to disgrace. He was almost fifty. But he seems to have held on to his money – there are records of a purchase of a substantial estate in Somerset – and he lived a literary life after that, known as an expert on Hinduism and all things Indian. He published a work on 'Mythology, Cosmogony, Fasts and Festivities of the Hinoos', 'Interesting Historical events relative to the Province of Bengal' and other writings of the same kind.

On his death, a fulsome obituary in *The Gentleman's Magazine* spoke of his 'brilliancy of talents, benignity of spirit, social vivacity and suavity of manners' and called him 'the most amiable of men'. Perhaps it was a merely formal expression; of all the traits history encourages us to associate with Holwell, amiability is not high on the list. His was obviously a flawed personality, and his honesty was always in question, but he must have been unusually brave and resourceful too.

Oddly enough, the greatest tribute to Holwell comes from no less a figure than Voltaire. In *Fragments historiques sur l'Inde*, the great writer honours the ex-surgeon's mate for his scholarship – 'we are grateful for the chance,' Voltaire writes,

to express the gratitude we owe to this man, who travelled the world purely in search of knowledge. He has revealed to us much that has remained hidden for centuries. We exhort whoever might wish to instruct themselves in the way that he did, to read these ancient allegorical fables, the prime sources of all the fables that have since provided deep truths in Persia, the Caldes, in Egypt and Greece . . .

It is rather fanciful – almost preposterous – to claim that Holwell's travels were entirely dedicated to intellectual pursuits, but Voltaire was scornfully intolerant of any discussion of trade or finance. 'These things' – he means Holwell's oriental researches – 'are more worthy of the study of the wise man than the quarrels of a few dealers about muslin and dyed cloth . . .'

Nevertheless, the muslin and dyed cloth had provided very well for Holwell's long retirement. He died in November 1798, at Pinner in Middlesex, at the age of eighty-seven.

10. Biography of a Phrase

Extracts from a letter from the Select Committee, Fort St George at Madras, to Admiral Watson, 13 November 1756:

We received late last night by the way of Bombay His Majesty's Declaration of War against France, which was enclosed to Mr Bourchier in a letter from the Secret Committee of the East India Company, and was proclaimed on the 17th May in England . . . If you judge the taking of Chandernagore practicable without much loss it would certainly be a step of great utility to the Company's affairs and take off in great measure the bad effects of the loss of Calcutta by putting the French in a position equally disadvantageous . . .

This letter reached Admiral Watson's hands as he set off from Madras with a naval fleet to accompany Robert Clive's land forces, their mission ostensibly to retake the Company's possessions in Bengal. It could hardly be a clearer statement of a moment when the collusion between commerce and politics became complete. With the formal declaration of hostilities in Europe, news that had taken six months to reach Madras, the line between the Company's affairs and the nation's affairs all but disappeared.

In theory, war or no war, the Company policy that explicitly discouraged the conquest or acquisition of territory was still in place. However, this was the moment when the Company realized, or was forced to realize, the truth about its own position, and to see that its posture as nothing but a large trading concern armed only in order to protect its commercial interests had become a fiction. Its attitude of mind – as John Keay describes it, one in which 'history was something that happened around them and to them . . . not something to which they contributed' – had to undergo a rapid change.

The change was partly an administrative one: although Clive's army were Company forces, Clive himself had a royal commission as a lieutenant-colonel, and Admiral Watson was in command of a squadron of the British navy, in a joint operation between government and commerce. This change was also brought on them by the new breed of Company servants, Robert Clive and others like him, young men who did not see that trade and empire-building could or should be kept separate. The logic was irrefutable. Political appeasement of local rulers inevitably slid into political intervention; the use of force for self-protection so easily led to its use in furthering one's own aims. And if logic was in favour of conquest, so were the talents and inclinations of the leading characters. Clive was still in his twenties, but already a decorated hero of Indian campaigns, rich through his own efforts, the darling of the Company (its chairman had presented him with a diamond-studded sword), lionized in the press and in London drawing rooms. Back in Madras after a spell in Britain, the 'news of the fall of Calcutta must have sounded like the muezzin of destiny', as Keay puts it. Clive was the obvious person to lead the expedition to Bengal, as he had both ability and experience, and it was certainly too good a challenge to resist. If the older Company men declined the call of history, even told themselves that they were mere businessmen who had no part in its course, Clive was the very opposite. In Robert Orme he had effectively a personal historian, a sort of political and military Boswell (he was also his partner in the inevitable private trade in which both were engaged). Clive not only knew that he was making history, but revelled in it. 'I am possessed of volumes of material [for you],' he wrote to Orme in 1757, 'in which will appear fighting, tricks, chicanery, intrigues, politics and the Lord knows what . . .'

Clive and Watson sailed north, and after a difficult voyage in which almost half the soldiers succumbed to disease, they entered the Hooghly in December 1756. Calcutta's refugees were still at Fulta, still living in dire circumstances on their ships and as best they could on land, but the arrival of the fleet from Madras was hugely encouraging. Perhaps also the arrival of men who clearly pulled rank on everyone else put an end to some of the petty in-fighting. Siraj was still flush with delight over his victory of the summer, extracting heavy fines from the French and the Dutch, comparing himself to Tamburlaine in letters to Delhi. Though Clive and Watson tried for a negotiation with Siraj – by an odd coincidence, the go-between was Warren Hastings, a man who would later become so famous in the history of the place but for now was a junior merchant caught in Kassimbazar – but the haughty nawab was impervious either to bribes or cajolery.

Just a month later, Clive's Madras sepoys, about 1,000 of them, marched up the Hooghly, while 800 European troops were carried upriver by Watson's fleet. After a muddled and inglorious but very speedy piece of military action, they retook Calcutta in January of 1757 without much difficulty – the only serious quarrel seemed to be between the two commanders, as Clive claimed the place for the Company and Watson claimed it for the Crown. When this little difficulty was overcome, in an unprecedented piece of joint action the newly restored Bengal Council actually published a declaration of war on Siraj, in the name of the East India Company, while Admiral Watson did the same in the name of the king.

This was a subterfuge of a sort. Battles against Siraj continued, but his affiliation with the French made it easier for Clive to move swiftly on to capture the large and important French settlement at Chandernagore in March. After a while, terms were made with Siraj-ud-daulah, in a treaty ensuring Calcutta's safety and freedom to trade, but his bitter hatred of the British was unappeased and he was still in bellicose mood. On 23 June 1757, he again mustered a large army – of about 50,000 – and went up against Clive's forces, which consisted of 800 Europeans and 2,200 Indians.

Plassey is a battle that has gone down in history as a magnificent military achievement. It was in fact an early example of match-fixing: Clive's achievements were impressive, but they were in the bargain-making rather than the soldierly sphere. He knew of the widespread dissatisfaction within Siraj's court, and he needed only to choose his target. He opened secret negotiations soon after his arrival in Bengal, and by the early summer he had already arranged with Siraj's uncle, Mir Jaffir, that he would be installed as Bengal's ruler after Siraj had been disposed of. Jaffir's supporters included prominent merchants who were suffering under Siraj's rackety rule; the battle of Plassey afforded the perfect opportunity for all sides. Siraj's clever general, Roy Dulabh, was also part of the arrangement, and during the battle itself he and his men barely lifted a finger. It is reckoned that only about a quarter of Siraj's troops stood by him.

After the battle the nawab fled, to be tracked down and murdered some days later in a grim and public humiliation. The British had lost sixty-five men; Clive received £234,000 from the grateful Mir Jaffir. With a puppet ruler whose aim was mutual advantage and enrichment, there was nothing to stop the British making Bengal their own. And if Plassey was only a great battle in the public relations version, its significance was great in another way, and its political repercussions were to be long-lasting.

It was not only Clive, with his huge personal 'gift' from the new nawab, who benefited from the agreement made with Mir Jaffir. Huge sums were allocated from the royal coffers as compensation for the loss of Calcutta, both to the Company and to individuals, to the Select Committee at Calcutta (whose members included the ubiquitous Watts and Drake) and to the army and the navy for their help. For Roy Dulabh's cooperation he had asked for 5 per cent of the treasure that had belonged to Siraj, and there were other debts that had to be settled – the Seths, for instance, demanded repayment of 700,000 rupees that had been owed to them by the French. It is a nice irony that now the British found themselves in the same position as Siraj had been at the fall of Calcutta – unpleasantly surprised by how little there was in the fabled piggy-bank, although the sums sound enormous to us. 'The scantiness of the Bengal treasury was most unexpected, as well as most painful news, to the English,' James Mill wrote, 'who had been accustomed to a fond and literal belief of oriental exaggeration on the subject of Indian riches.' But there was money enough, apparently, in the nawab's treasury – even though there were some suspicious dealings too – and it gave Clive a good deal of satisfaction to calculate that as much as £4.5 million had been paid out altogether. In this 'Revolution', he claimed, every subaltern would benefit to the tune of £3,000. Large grants of land went to the Company, as well: it was another step on the way to becoming a colonial, rather than a purely financial, power. The East India Company had done very nicely in the end out of the loss of Calcutta, and, as Hill put it, with some sarcasm, 'thus, by the generosity of Mir Jaffir, the sufferings of the British in Bengal seemed to have been swept away like an evil dream, and for the moment all was triumph and satisfaction'.

The famous painting of Clive and Mir Jaffir after the battle of Plassey is easy enough to decode. On the left of the picture, the uniformed Clive and his officers, and a wild-eyed and rearing horse; on the right, Mir Jaffir and his attendants and a vast elephant – a creature which, despite its size, is far more placid than the westerners' animal. If the elephant is India, immense and exotic but easily kept in check by one small mahout, the noble horse with its flaring nostrils and its only-just-contained menace symbolizes the incomers' power. The body-language of the principals is eloquent, too: although the painting purports to show a meeting of equals, Mir Jaffir is slightly bent over, in just the suggestion of homage, his hands outstretched in a submissive or at least placatory gesture, making Clive the taller of the two.

After Plassey, Clive was appointed to the governership of Bengal. Perhaps because there was a quarrel, perhaps just to ensure his power over the nawab, Clive quite soon deposed Mir Jaffir and installed his son-in-law Mir Kasim on the throne, but this did not last long, and Clive reinstated Mir Jaffir when Kasim showed a tendency to too much independence. His dominion over the court was uncontested.

The dispatching of Siraj, the installation of a safe puppet ruler in Bengal and the restoration of trade at Calcutta were not Clive's only aims, however. He had his eye on much more. Flushed with success after yet another military victory, at Buxar in 1764, he wrote the famously intemperate letter in which he describes the Indians as 'indolent, luxurious, ignor-ant and cowardly beyond all conception'; he tells his masters in London that if they would provide him with 2,000 well-trained European troops, then he could 'secure our present acquisitions or improve upon them' in a way that 'leaves nothing to the power of [the Indians'] treachery or ingrati-tude'. In other words, Bengal was theirs for the taking. At the same time, he was covered himself with his employers by seeming to agree with their standpoint: 'an influence main-tained by force of arms was destructive of that commercial spirit which the servants of the Company ought to promote,' he wrote, 'oppressive to the country and ruinous to the Company; whose military expenses had hitherto rendered fruitless their extraordinary success, and even the cession of rich provinces'.

In fact, this argument tended – as he knew – not away from conquest but towards it. If military action was ruinous to trade, then if negotiations failed the only real alternative was to ensure a peaceful atmosphere by force. The logic had become inexorable.

The decisive shift took place in a more dignified way than the mighty drum-roll Clive had in mind. At the Treaty of Allahabad in 1765 came what could be seen as the final turning point in the journey towards full imperial rule by Britain: the Mughal emperor granted to the East India Company the *diwani* – that is, the civil administration – of Bengal, Orissa and Bihar. It was, as Niall Ferguson puts it, 'a license not to print money but the next best thing: to raise it in taxation'. Some 20 million people fell under the jurisdiction of the British, and from them they could claim tax revenues of somewhere between £2 and £3 million a year. A letter was dispatched to Leadenhall Street that was for once completely unequivocal in its language. 'You,' the Directors were informed, 'are now become the sovereigns of a rich and potente kingdome.'

P. J. Marshall puts it more calmly. 'Effective authority transferred to the East India Company in 1765,' he writes. 'The foundations of territorial empire had been laid.' Marshall also investigates the process in a way less dramatic than those historians who like to quote Clive writing to his father promising that he had 'come to do great things'. 'At a time when the Company's Indian trade was relatively stagnant,' he explains, 'the case for trying to bring about a more favourable commercial environment through political intervention seemed to be an attractive one.' He points out that Bengal was not hard to govern: it had a skilled bureaucracy and a centralized structure, it had a banking system and sophisticated trading networks – far from being a ragtag collection of villages and tribes it was a 'centralized indigenous state' over which the British could impose authority with 'relative ease'. The move from 'expansion' to 'empire' had begun.

The Company's greatest triumph was perhaps simultaneously the beginning of its end. It administered the growing British territories in India without much interference for only a few more years, until in 1773 the Regulating Act passed by parliament curtailed its power considerably. In 1784, the 25-year-old prime minister, William Pitt, the grandson of 'Diamond' Pitt, passed the India Act, which established dual control of the East India Company and centralized British rule in India by reducing the power of the governors of Bombay and Madras and increasing that of the governor-general, and putting policy in the hands of a Board of Control answerable to parliament. The Company continued to exist and trade and wield a certain influence, although increasingly riven by financial scandal and challenged by a plethora of other trade networks; it was not until 1857, after the Mutiny, that Queen Victoria could claim with great excitement 'that India should belong to *me*'.

Calcutta rose from its ashes with extraordinary speed. Within fifteen or twenty years after the Black Hole and the surrender to Siraj-ud-daulah, its river banks were 'studded with elegant mansions . . . surrounded by grass and lawns, and present a constant succession of whatever can delight the eye, or bespeak wealth and elegance in the owners', in the words of Eliza Fay. In 1789 a Mughal visitor, Abdul Lateef Shushtari, was overwhelmed by the sight of some 5,000 imposing two- or three-storeyed houses of stone or brick or stucco, good drains, efficient street-cleaning and safety from robbers – more than most large European cities could boast at the same date – as well as the awe-inspiring sight of 1,000 ships at anchor in the river. Thomas Twining, who arrived in 1792, sailing up the Hooghly, describes the Esplanade that separated the *maidan* and the new fort from the city.

A range of magnificent buildings, including the Governor's Palace, the Council House, the Supreme Court House, the Accountant General's Office, etc., extended eastward from the river, and then turning at a right angle to the south, formed the limit of both the city and the plain. Nearly all these buildings were occupied by civil and military officers of the Government, either as their public offices or private residences. They were all white, their roofs invariably flat, surrounded by colonnades, and their fronts relieved by lofty columns, supporting lofty verandahs. They were all separated from each other, each having its own small enclosure, in which the kitchen, the cellars, storerooms, etc. were at a little distance from the house, and a large folding gate and porter's lodge at the entrance.

Twining had also spotted Garden Reach, the city's residential quarters:

Handsome villas lined the left or southern bank, and on the opposite shore there was the residence of the Superintendent of the Company's botanical gardens. It was a large upper-roomed house not many yards from the river, along the edge of which the garden itself extended. The situation of the elegant garden houses, as the villas on the left bank were called, surrounded by verdant grounds laid out in the English style, with the Ganges flowing before them, struck me as singularly beautiful.

Calcutta had become the largest and most splendid colonial city in India and quickly gained a reputation for being the most dissipated, too.

But while this transformation was going on, there were murmurs of dissatisfaction on two sides. At home in London, after Plassey, even the most hard-nosed among the Company's directors was shocked by the outrageous profits made in the service of a foreign monarch by men who were, after all, supposed to be working for the Company. To put Clive's personal booty into perspective: of his £234,000 he spent just £10,000 on a house in Berkeley Square and £70,000 on a huge estate in Shropshire. When he faced a committee of inquiry, however, he made his famous remark: 'I stand astonished at my own moderation.' The morality of this was a difficult call: the Company deliberately paid very low wages on the understanding that their position gave men the chance to make personal fortunes by trade, and at the time it was not a disgrace for gentlemen to be paid for their services by noblemen. Even so, there were questions asked about the British officers' motives in going to war with Siraj – was Plassey a battle purely for profit? – and the taint of financial misdealings dogged Clive until the end of his life, when such glory foundered in depression and suicide.

At the same time, the Bengalis had seen their country slide inexorably into the possession of foreigners who only a short time earlier had been merely tolerated as merchants. As each new wave of traders arrived, their greed increased, and for a time the British seemed to see Bengal as nothing but a treasure trove to be looted with all speed. As the memory of Mughal misrule faded, these new overlords came to appear just as rapacious, and according to one contemporary source 'the people looked with greater and greater dislike on their new rulers'. S. C. Hill published his history of Bengal in 1905, when the Indian Civil Service, whose strictly disinterested and selfless codes of practice dated back to the Cornwallis Code of 1793, had already been in place for half a century, so his conclusion needs to be seen in the context of late-

Victorian distrust of the profit motive as a basis for government when he declares rather pompously that 'a great nation
does not properly safeguard its honour when it places its
dealings with foreigners in the hands of men who are servants
of a trading Company'.

This mercenary motive for the taking of parts of India, and
the expansion of colonized-for-profit territories that now
began in earnest, was a 'taint' – his word – that would take a
long time to eradicate.

It is open to doubt whether even now [i.e. 1905] the natives of
Bengal are able to appreciate at anything like their full value either
the benefit they received by the liberation of the country from the
tyranny of Siraj-ud-daulah, or the disinterestedness of so much of
the work done since then by the servants first of the East India
Company and then of the British crown.

This has vivid echoes across a neat time-span of 100 years.
The talk of liberation from Siraj and tyranny (when Hill
knew perfectly well that the motive at the time was entirely
economic and self-interested); the complaint of not being
appreciated by the people whose country you have taken
over – this resonates closely with the situation in Iraq in 2005.
By the time of Hill's remarks, Calcutta was at the height of
its beauty and sophistication, still the capital of British India,
its resplendent Government House occupied by Lord Curzon
as viceroy, and his great buildings in the city gleaming new.
During the previous century it had been nicknamed the City
of Palaces, and not all those palaces were in foreign hands.
The Marble Palace on Muktaram Babu Street, built in 1835
by Raja Rajendro Mullick in a shining fusion of eastern and
western styles, and housing a collection of both oriental and
western works of art, is probably the best known of the

magnificent houses built by Indian families who had become fabulously rich through the coming of the foreign trade.

But to say that under foreign domination some Indians prospered enormously – and perhaps a great many prospered a little – is beside the point. The century between S. C. Hill and ourselves is the time in which thinking about colonialism has changed so fundamentally that we have to make a mental shift to appreciate what he is saying, and what his contemporaries believed. We need to make this leap to understand what value the story of the Black Hole had for them. Whereas most people now believe that the domination by force of another country – however many benefits might be brought to that country – is unacceptable, that was not usually true in 1905. The British were perhaps peculiar in administering their empire on strict tenets of service and lack of personal gain – the Indian civil servants, as if in reaction to the buccaneers of the East India Company that went before them, were not allowed to trade at all in India, not even to own a small parcel of land. They were salaried employees who considered themselves incorruptible, and the overwhelming majority of them were. They had other goals. The notion of service was paramount, and it was service to the British Crown, of course, but the concept of serving India and her people was not far behind, especially by the early part of the twentieth century, when the ICS admitted a large number of Indians into its ranks.

That the vast millions of India could be dominated and run by a few thousand British people has been considered extraordinary, as it was. Perhaps it could only have been done by a nation with a certain idea of itself. What was needed was supreme self-confidence, the apparently unshakeable kind that has long been a defining characteristic of the USA. And for that kind of national sense, a country needs its defining myths and legends around which to cluster as if they were so many flagpoles.

The Black Hole of Calcutta became one of these legends, and in the history of India it was joined, a century later, by other pulse-points of national feeling: the Mutiny, the well at Cawnpore, the siege of Lucknow. In modern minds these events melt more or less into one – it is rare to find someone now who knows that the Black Hole pre-dates the Mutiny by a century. It is interesting – and typically British, maybe – that the most powerful defining myths were not great victories, they were usually stories of hardship and defeat or even horror and atrocity overcome with pride and grit: what is known as the Dunkirk spirit. Attack and adversity contribute to national cohesion in a way that success and affluence do not. George Monbiot recently took this idea even further by saying that:

the more powerful a nation becomes, the more it asserts its victimhood. In contemporary British eyes, the greatest atrocities of the 18th and 19th centuries were those perpetrated on compatriots in the Black Hole of Calcutta or during the Indian mutiny and the siege of Khartoum. The extreme manifestations of the white man's burden, these events came to symbolise the barbarism and ingratitude of the savage races the British had sought to rescue from their darkness.

The other problem about the Black Hole, as a story of heroism and self-sacrifice to a cause, is that it was not either of those things. There was precious little altruism to be found anywhere in this story. Yet the necessary heroism of young men like Henry Lushington or Ensign Piccard was unfortunately not exceptional in the history of the times: these young men came to trade, but were forced to fight, more often by the foolishness of their own colleagues than by the aggression of others. Such remarkable valour hardly shows up in the pages of history, however, except in the heart-rending inscriptions and memorials that are found in country churches all over England, where grieving parents got their only chance to say goodbye. A good story was needed, or at least a story that blurred any of the details that did not fit. And that is perhaps why the legend became more useful when more time had elapsed and the emotive phrase itself spread its wings to obscure any inconvenient realities that might linger in the memory.

At the time Holwell's account was published in London, there was scandal and horror. The details of what happened that terrible night were repeated with relish, together with whispered embellishments, but the striking thing about the late eighteenth-century reports is that the fall of Calcutta, rather than the Black Hole itself, was what was important in the public mind. Perhaps every historical milestone that settles firmly into the popular imagination does so because of its good luck in having a memorable name – the Boston Tea Party, the Battle of Wounded Knee – and the Black Hole is among the best of them. Thus, slowly, the Black Hole took over, and even in quite scrupulous sources we find it recorded that someone suffered or died in the Black Hole, when in fact it was at some point during the siege and capture of Calcutta, or its aftermath. The Black Hole, as a phrase, became a shorthand not only for all that happened at Calcutta, but for what can go suddenly wrong in times of apparent ease and prosperity. Charles Stewart, writing in 1813, joined the army of hyperbolists when he claimed that 'the capture of Fort William, and the sufferings of its inhabitants, strongly evince the fallacy of all human speculations', a pretty ridiculous claim when one examines it, but typical of the kind of language that was used about the event from the start.

Gradually, over the years, the phrase became more resonant

as an image of fear, rather than evoking Stewart's more lofty philosophical associations. It is about the fear of blackness; the existential fear of the unknown, of nothingness, of being lost and helpless in an unfathomable deep; but more specifically a fear of savagery and what Foucault called 'the other'. The 'black' in Black Hole originally had nothing to do with race, and referred only to the darkness of the cell, but its later echoes cannot escape a racial connotation.

The early version, of sacrifice and heroism, lasted a surprisingly long time. When Noel Barber published his account in 1965, he began by saying, 'Every schoolboy knows about the Black Hole of Calcutta, or believes he does, for it appears in the history curriculum as regularly as the battle of Hastings or the South Sea Bubble.' Forty years on, it is probably safe to say that very few schoolboys know about the Black Hole of Calcutta, except possibly in Calcutta, where a version of the episode was taught in schools until fairly recently, although it has now disappeared both from the curriculum, and, largely, from the city's memory. In Britain it does still appear in some history curricula, but only as a 'What really happened?' question. The authorized version, as laid down for almost 250 years and reheated time and again in such classics as *Our Island Story*, is embarrassing in a multi-cultural, post-colonial atmosphere.

It is probably because of the upsetting connotations of the phrase that the event has provoked such acid controversy. In the great sweep of eighteenth-century history, even if the focus is narrowed down just to India, and then just to Bengal, and then just to Calcutta, surely it hardly matters whether there were 123 deaths, or six. No one is counting so precisely for the thousands who died in the rest of the conflict. And even if we admit the horrible truth, that when history belongs to the victors their dead count for more than other people's dead, the arguments over the Black Hole still don't quite make sense. There is no acrimonious numbers game played about, for instance, the number of British people who died of wounds and fever during the seven months they spent huddled in Fulta, but it was probably about the same number as perished in the Black Hole.

This perpetual bargaining over numbers is not about numbers. It is about motives. It is about whether a deliberate act of atrocity can be ascribed to Siraj – clearly it cannot, and everyone who looks at the records seems to agree that in this case he was guilty of nothing more than carelessness. It is about whether the British had any justification in using the episode as a springboard for the expansion some of them anyway wanted, and for using force to gain what they had previously gained by negotiation. And it is about the way in which these legendary episodes cast the native rulers and their people as savages.

Holwell did not invent his story about what happened in the Black Hole. Those who claim that he did – J. H. Little was not the first, but he was the most extreme when he described the whole saga as 'a hoax' – cannot seem to account for the corroborating evidence from other survivors. Holwell could not have fixed that; the people were across the world from each other, and sometimes they were writing in a spirit of hostility to each other rather than a spirit of collusion. But it seems certain that he exaggerated. Practically, it would have been impossible to count the number of people in that cell, in the pitch dark and with such crowding that bodies were on top of one another. What is suspicious is his attempt at certainty. All the accounts agree that nobody counted how many went in to the cell, and nobody was going to stop to count the corpses the next morning. Even the tally of survivors, although it is the most reliable figure, is far from precise. What is noticeable is that every version of the story uses a sort of filmic technique: the panning shots never linger on the details of the bigger picture, but always pull the focus in quickly to highlight a few individuals. No one has ever been able to name more than a couple of dozen victims, and although these people obviously did die, there is no proof that they died in the Black Hole that night.

Most of Holwell's critics accuse him of self-aggrandizement, of wanting to be a hero and to gain promotion in the Company – some of the Calcutta survivors, indeed, did get bumped a grade or two up the career ladder, 'for good behaviour'. And Holwell returned to Calcutta as governor, a huge promotion, although he soon got on the wrong side of Clive and became ensnared in some tricky financial dealings that led to his resignation from the Company. Nevertheless, he succeeded: he lived a very prosperous retirement and died at an extraordinary age; history knows his name, on the whole with a favourable ring to it, and even in 1966 he found in Barber a passionate champion.

There could, however, have been another powerful motive for Holwell's urge to augment the numbers of victims. After he took over, on the desertion of Drake and the others, there was a degree of chaos that was far worse than it need have been. Holwell could have saved a lot of lives if he had surrendered immediately. He probably did have dreams of glory when he urged the settlement to fight on; the result was a huge loss of life. It is likely that Holwell knew he would have to account for many of these deaths – for John Bellamy and his old father, for Peter Carey, for Clayton, for Eyre, for Thomas Cole and Captain Buchanan and the hopeless Witherington, for Jencks and Law and Jebb and many more – and would be blamed for them if it were shown that they were caused by his bad judgement. Perhaps they sat heavily on his conscience. So when he realized he had a perfect opportunity to locate these deaths heroically and pitifully in the cell that night, rather than brutally and pointlessly on the battlements or the parade ground earlier that day, Holwell took his chance and wrote his narrative.

Others may well have taken their chance, too. There is a Captain P. Smith recorded among the deserters to Fulta, but he appears as a Black Hole victim on one of the lists: given that the survivors had necessarily to compare notes, and some prominent commentators such as Mills and Grey were not in the Black Hole at all, it was quite possible that Smith helped to make up the casualty list on which his own name appeared. It could have been a neat escape from bad debts, a bad marriage, or a number of other circumstances.

It is a perfect example of the way in which history belongs to the survivors – for a while. One Indian commentator has written that 'for the British it became an article of faith to accept the veracity of the episode in its most extravagant and sordid form', which is another way of saying that Holwell's self-protective narrative just happened to chime perfectly with what the larger forces of the situation demanded: a strong story to pluck at the heart-strings at home and stiffen the sinews of conquest and empire abroad. It was useful at the time and it remained useful – in odd manifestations – for a long time. The oddest, perhaps, is that when the journalist Fiammetta Rocco was a girl at school in what was then Rhodesia in the early 1970s, the Christmas play put on every year by her smart, all-white girls' school in that black country was a fictionalized re-enactment of the Black Hole of Calcutta.

The phrase itself passed into the everyday use of British people who had no idea what really happened in Calcutta, but still pick up on its resonance to describe anything from an airless office to a crowded bus. One finds it everywhere: the American writer Martha Gellhorn used it in her description of a field hospital in Normandy in 1940. The term is out of date now, and most people under thirty have little idea what it refers to, or think it is a phenomenon in outer space. But for those who are slightly older, it still comes in handy on a regular basis. One classical music critic, Anthony Holden, has used it to describe London's Albert Hall on a warm night three times in three Proms seasons. In 2005 alone, Sheridan Morley wrote that backstage conditions at the King's Head theatre in Islington 'made the Black Hole of Calcutta resemble a five-star hotel', and Simon Hoggart described the *Guardian* office in the House of Commons as 'a space so tiny that it makes the Black Hole of Calcutta seem like a Dorchester suite'. There are thousands of other such quotes: the phrase is enjoying a ripe old age, applied to everything from ill-lit basements to teenagers' bedrooms.

These authors are British men of the age to have learnt their school history with a strongly imperial spice. In the realms of post-colonial academic thought, no one would want to use the phrase so lightly, or with a quasi-comic turn. It turns up, oddly again, in Thomas Pynchon's novel *Mason & Dixon*, when his narrator, the Reverend Cherrycoke, views the Black Hole of Calcutta as a 'retaliatory metaphor' of the 'continental coercion' that is the British practice in India: a light spoofing of the sometimes over-serious terminology of political sensitivities.

The political sensitivities were real enough in Calcutta, however. Just as the Black Hole had been a powerful myth for the Empire, it was equally significant for its opponents. When the nationalist leader Subhas Chandra Bose staged demonstrations in Calcutta in 1940, often at the foot of the Black Hole monument, which was then still standing proudly at the corner of Calcutta's busiest square, the British authorities were forced to take action. In a letter of July that year from Sir John Herbert to Lord Linlithgow, the viceroy, Herbert reminds his boss how potent and provocative a symbol Lord Curzon's white marble obelisk had proved to be.

The story of the monument reveals a good deal about the changes in thinking about empire and about the British in India. Holwell first erected his brick and plaster obelisk, inscribed with about fifty names, of those who died both in the siege of Calcutta and in the Black Hole itself, when he returned to the city in 1758. He put it on the site of the ditch in which the bodies had been so roughly buried that June morning, a memorial and a gravestone. As the city grew, the square that contained the Great Tank became its centre, first called Tank Square, then Dalhousie Square, before its name was changed to Binoy, Badal, Dinesh Bagh (always known as BBD Bagh) after three brothers who laid siege to the Writers' Building and were later killed during the independence struggles. The monument stood at the north-west angle, its most visible: in front of the large new Writers' Building, directly in the sight-line of two of Calcutta's largest avenues.

The weather took its toll, as ever, and the monument began to crumble and rot, and there seemed little interest in its preservation; on 6 April 1821, the *Calcutta Journal* records its demolition and removal. A few days later, on 11 April, a columnist who signed himself 'Britannicus' called this 'an act of sacrilege', but he seems to have been a lone voice. For eighty years after that, there was nothing to record or mark the Black Hole and its victims.

When Clive recaptured Calcutta in 1757, there were some attempts to restore the fort – attacks by the French were more of a concern now. It was a temporary measure, though, while the large and far more powerfully armoured new one – also called Fort William – was constructed 2 miles to the south, close to the river, on land specially cleared and drained from the jungle. It stands today, in the middle of a parkland of many acres, a *maidan* that was deliberately made to enable the fort's cannon to find their range. The lesson of the bunched-up houses had been well learnt. But the remains of the old fort were still in use, as warehouses and offices, for many years, its demolition long past the planned date. When the watercolourist Thomas Daniell visited Calcutta in 1786, he could see enough of the old fort to paint it in some detail, but it was effectively a ruin. Pieces of the south wall remained for another century, until in 1895 Calcutta's main post office, an imposing building that occupies the whole city block, with a gleaming white dome, a pillared entrance with wide steps and a lofty central hall, was built on the site. Apparently some underground parts of the old fort were left underneath, and one writer records that in 1902 Post Office employees had their tiffin room next to a sunken arcade used to store the Post Office wagons, of which two arched sections were closed in and used as a kitchen. The space made like that was probably a bit larger than the Black Hole had been, but it would have been easy to imagine.

This was something Lord Curzon saw, when he set about his memorial project and went to inspect the site in February of 1900. On his voyage to India as newly appointed viceroy little more than a year earlier, in December of 1898, Curzon had read H. E. Busteed's *Echoes from Old Calcutta* in one of its early editions (he provides a letter of preface to later ones, in which he calls the book 'both a romance and an inspiration'). In it, he read the detailed story of the Black Hole, an incident he would probably have known from school history books in his boyhood, but which may now have struck him with new force. It may also have been the moment at which he learnt that there was no memorial or marker of any kind. The romance and the inspiration both stayed with him, and he conceived for Calcutta, a place he saw as 'one great graveyard of memories', what he later described as 'a policy to which I have deliberately set myself in India – namely, that of preserving, in a breathless and often thoughtless age, the relics and memorials of the past'. According to his biographer David Gilmour, 'within weeks of his arrival [in Calcutta] he had informed [Sir John] Woodburn of his intention to restore the Old Fort and to rebuild at his own expense the monument to the victims of the Black Hole'.

Woodburn was the lieutenant governor of Bengal; soon Curzon was corresponding with London on the subject too. Given everything else the viceroy had to do, his enthusiasm and attention to the details of the project are impressive. One letter of the time ranges across the Transvaal War, policy in Persia, a case of rape by soldiers in Rangoon, famine relief in India (he records an incredible 790,000 people 'upon public works'), British war office decentralization – and still finds time for discussion of Holwell's monument. It must have been a project close to Curzon's heart.

London did not see it in the same light. On the contrary: stiff resistance came from the India Office, in letters from Sir Arthur Godley, the under-secretary. The mood was 'very averse to re-erecting this obelisk', he wrote, because of the message it might convey: 'parading our disaster and the consequences which ensued [could have] a very bad effect on the Native mind'. Curzon countered by saying that if that were so, then he would have to remove the marble angel that commemorated the masscare at Cawnpore: the argument simmered on.

It is interesting that the powerful viceroy felt he had to ask permission for something as small as the putting up of a single monument, even though what he was proposing involved the demolition of another statue on the site, one in which 'Sir Ashley Eden sits in a grotesque marble chair', as he put it. But no one seemed to care very much about Sir Ashley, and in the end there was no stopping Curzon. His offer to pay for the new monument personally probably helped, as did his plea that it was all part of a overall idea of 'placing in Calcutta some memorials of its wonderfully dramatic past' and a promise to 'eliminate invidious expressions' on the inscription. The Council waived their objections, before long, on the understanding that it must be seen as 'part of a scheme for the decoration of Calcutta'.

But even if the authorities were comforting themselves with the thought that this was mere 'decoration', Curzon was not so coy about its political significance. He was quite specific, in letters and speeches, about the role he felt the Black Hole and its victims had played in the foundation of the Raj, and the reasons why a memorial was so necessary. The phrases roll out with all Curzon's usual eloquence, and more than a touch of high emotion. 'The fact that their death was practically the foundation-stone of the British Empire in India,' he wrote to Godley, 'invests their memory with particular historical importance.' A letter to S. C. Hill in the Records Department asks him to investigate the names of those 'who took part in those historic events which established the British dominion in Bengal'. And again, in the speech he gave at the new monument's unveiling, on 19 December 1902, he honours the 'martyr band', these 'ancient and unconscious builders of Empire', 'the brave men whose life-blood had cemented the foundations of the British Empire in India'.

It is possible that, if it had not been for Lord Curzon, the Black Hole episode would have sunk into oblivion and its victims, the 'authors of a wonderful chapter in the history of Mankind', completely forgotten. The nineteenth century had not cared much for its memory: there were aspects of it that many in the Victorian era found uncomfortable. A few enthusiasts had worked on excavations in the 1870s, but the last person who records actually seeing the prison cell itself was the writer Asiaticus, who visited in 1812 when the final demolition of the old fort was supposed to begin. Other literary visitors paid it little attention – even Louis de Grandpré, the French traveller who left such vivid accounts of his Indian experience, and who visited Calcutta in 1787, only thirty-one years after 'the troubles', gives us only a sort of gossipy version, presumably one that was current in Calcutta at the time: that the prisoners had been 'thrust upon one another into a hole outside the fort' and only the few who had been at the top survived. Presumably it was generally believed, by this time, that Holwell's monument stood over the 'Hole' itself.

Through these layers of confusion and indifference, Curzon had considerable work to do, by 1900, to unearth the facts. He organized archaeologists to excavate the burial site (they found nothing) and what could be investigated on the site of the fort; he corresponded with Busteed and S. C. Hill in London and T. R. Munro in Edinburgh about the identity of the victims and the survivors. Their research was detailed: they checked widows' pension petitions to the East India Company; the bill for wages due to Thomas Leach, the carpenter, sent in after his death by his family; an account submitted by the executors of William Baillie for cloth, bandages and cartridges supplied during the siege. The list of victims' names available for the viceregal memorial was longer than that on the original (sixty, compared to Holwell's forty-eight) and Curzon congratulates himself on this in one of the careful inscriptions, adding that 'the additional names, and the Christian names of the remainder, have been recovered from oblivion by reference to contemporary documents'. Despite the best efforts of this research, though, the list is not very much more reliable: like all the previous attempts at a full list, it has to rely on other accounts and it compounds their mistakes. For instance, in the second edition of Busteed's book the ever-mysterious Eleanor Weston was listed as the mother of Peter Carey, rather than of Mary (although this was probably not accurate either), and Curzon must have accepted that version.

The monument is bigger and grander than the original, whose dimensions Curzon 'found to be rather stunted' in juxtaposition to the tall buildings around the site. It is finely carved with the wreaths and cherubs' heads about which Curzon sent instructions to a local engineer: no trouble or expense was spared. And this grand obelisk was not all. As well as the monument itself, and the black marble slab set into the ground as near as possible on the site of the Black Hole itself, Curzon also ordered about a dozen white marble tablets to be placed on various parts of the walls of the Post Office, inside and out, with details of what part of the old fort it corresponded to, and how far from the site of the Black Hole it would have been. Finally, a brass line was set into the stone of the steps of the Post Office, tracing the edge of the south bastion of the fort. Of all these many memorials, this brass line is the only one that remains in place and can be seen now – although it is tarnished and faded beneath the dust of myriad feet.

The speech Curzon gave at the unveiling of his 'personal gift to the city of Calcutta', on 19 December 1902, makes great reading. It contains everything: his easy style, his wonderfully rolling and emotive phrases and the clever politician's ability to please and placate. 'If there should be a spot that should be dear to British in India,' one can imagine him thundering sonorously, 'it is that below our feet which was stained with the blood and which closed over the victims that night of destiny, 20th June 1756.' But even at such a moment of personal and political triumph Curzon balances his account. Imperial history, he says, 'is often a chronicle of errors and blunders and crimes, but it also abounds in the records of virtue and heroism and valour'. The vocabulary of this speech is interesting: the word 'blood' comes up several times – the 'life-blood that cemented the foundations of Empire', and so on – and it is no surprise to find 'virtue', 'heroism' and 'valour', but it is more surprising to find mention of blunders and even crimes. He is anxious to tell his listeners that in his memorial projects he is 'equally keen about preserving relics of Hindu and Muselman, of Brahman and Buddhist, of Dravidian and Pathan'. And in contrast to the highly charged language of the speech, the inscriptions, although detailed, are restrained; there is nothing set in stone about martyrdom or destiny or life-blood or the building of empire. One of his spoken comments underlines this cautious approach:

Holwell's inscription, written by himself with the memory of that awful experience still fresh in his mind, contained a bitter reference to the personal responsibility for the tragedy of Siraj-ud-daulah, which I think is not wholly justified by our fuller knowledge of the facts . . . I have therefore struck [it] out as calculated to keep alive feelings that we should all wish to see die.

Curzon's attempts to placate nationalist feelings and Muslim feelings were pretty much in vain, however. The Black Hole story was not only a potentially explosive one for Indian nationalists, but played into sectarian passions as well. It offended Muslims because it imputed extreme cruelty, if not actually genocidal tendencies, to Siraj, and within only a few years they were condemning 'the falsity of foreign historians' and urging the deletion of the Black Hole incident from all schoolbooks. Still today, on websites and in articles, the sectarian aspects of the story arouse strong feelings. With his elaborate memorial Curzon had indeed created the 'perpetual remembrance of the past' he had wanted – but perhaps not the one that he intended.

'Agitation for removal of this monument has occurred from time to time since 1938,' Sir John Herbert wrote to Lord Linlithgow, the viceroy, in 1940. 'One of the constant endeavours of Subhash Bose and the Forward Bloc [has been] to find some plank on which civil disobedience can be started with the assistance of Moslems.'

Curzon's monument provided just the right 'plank' for the nationalists to enlist Muslims. Herbert was trying to persuade Bose not to carry out a planned *satyagraha*, a sit-down protest that was unlikely to stay sitting down for long and would almost certainly erupt into an episode of serious civil violence, and he was particularly concerned at the skill with which Bose could manipulate this piece of monumental architecture, and all that it stood for, to his cause. Even in the relatively formal tone of the letter, Herbert sounds rattled. He wants to get rid of the monument, as soon as possible: he knew its power, just as Curzon had known it. Day and night, the great white prong that dominated the heart of the city seemed to thumb its nose at the nationalists and all they stood for. He used any argument he could muster to persuade Linlithgow to allow the dismantling of his illustrious predecessor's work, including the strange one (in such a new-built city) that the monument was 'not of archaeological interest' because it was not Holwell's brick and plaster original, but a mere reproduction. The fact that the second monument was far more splendid and explicit than the first only compounded its problematic status.

Herbert pleaded for its removal to 'a disused cemetery or any other reasonable place', and before long he managed to get the European community in Calcutta to agree to its change of location, 'for the sake of the general goodwill'.

Thus Curzon's Black Hole monument retained its symbolic power throughout; what its maker probably could not have foreseen was how quickly, and utterly, that symbolism would go into reverse. Nor that his beautifully built marble would stay in place for less time than Holwell's gimcrack pukka. It was installed at the height of imperial splendour and self-confidence, as a tribute to the men who had begun to make all that magnificence come about, but also as a reminder. It was a totem-pole for the faithful of empire. As such, it could only enrage the nationalists, and its relegation was also a powerful symbol. It stands now in a far corner of the messy garden of St John's church, on Council House Street. In another part of the graveyard where Job Charnock is buried, and Begum Johnson (the legendary Calcutta matron who was formerly the Mrs Watts of the siege at Kassimbazar), the church where Thackeray's parents were married, the church painted by Zoffany and the Daniells brothers, where monuments that speak of the exploits of the daring and the quieter lives of the timid encrust the walls.

From Job Charnock, in his Mughal-style mausoleum, to Curzon's obsolete thrusting symbol: the whole of Calcutta's imperial history seems to be contained in this one church and its graveyard. The inscriptions on the sides of the Black Hole monument are almost impossible to read now: although no weather will ever blunt the pristine lines of the lavish marble carving, simpler forces of moss and dirt and neglect, as well as the waist-high nettles around the monument's base, are more prosaic barriers to a casual passer-by. The moss and the nettles seem to say it all.

The last word in this story should probably go to Holwell. Pulling every hyperbole off the shelf, he summed up what had happened at Calcutta as 'as fatal and melancholy a catastrophe as ever the annals of any people, or colony of people, suffered since the days of Adam'. But the real last word will go to Nirad Chaudhuri, who in a single phrase encapsulated the effects of this 'catastrophe': 'it threw a moral halo over the British conquest of India'.

Select Bibliography

Barber, Noel: *The Black Hole of Calcutta: A Reconstruction*, Collins 1965.

Busteed, H. E.: *Echoes from Old Calcutta*, 4th edition, London 1905.

Cannadine, David: *Ornamentalism: How the British Saw Their Empire*, Allen Lane 2001.

Colley, Linda: *Britons*, Yale University Press 1992.

Colley, Linda: *Captives: Britain, Empire and the World 1600–1850*, Jonathan Cape 2002.

Cotton, Evan and Fawcett, Charles: *East Indiamen: The East India Company's Maritime Service*, Batchworth Press 1949.

Dalrymple, William: *White Mughals: Love and Betrayal in 18th-century India*, HarperCollins 2002.

De, Amalendu: 'A Note on the Black Hole Tragedy', *Quarterly Review of Historical Studies*, X, 3 and 4 (1970–71).

Fay, Eliza: *The Original Letters from India of Mrs Eliza Fay*, Thacker and Spink 1903.

Ferguson, Niall: *The Cash Nexus: Money and Power in the Modern World 1700–2000*, Allen Lane 2001.

Ferguson, Niall: *Empire: How Britain Made the Modern World*, Allen Lane 2003.

Gilmour, David: *Curzon*, John Murray 1994.

Gilmour, David: *The Ruling Caste: Imperial Lives in the Victorian Raj*, John Murray 2005.

Gupta, Brijen K.: *The Black Hole Incident*, E. J. Brill 1959.

Gupta, Brijen K.: *Sirajuddaullah and the East India Company, 1756–1757: Background to the Foundation of British Power in India*, E. J. Brill 1966.

Hickey, William: *Memoirs*, Hutchinson 1960.

Hill, S. C.: *Bengal in 1756–1757*, London, 1905.

Holwell, John Zephaniah: *A Genuine Narrative of the Deplorable Deaths of the English Gentlemen and Others who were Suffocated in the Black Hole*, London, 1758.

Holwell, John Zephaniah: *Indian Tracts*, London 1764.

Holwell, John Zephaniah: *Interesting Historical Events Relative to the Provinces of Bengal and the Empire of Indostan*, London 1772.

James, Lawrence: *Rise and Fall of the British Empire*, Abacus 1995.

Jasanoff, Maya: *Edge of Empire*, Fourth Estate 2005.

Keay, John: *The Honourable Company: History of the East India Company*, HarperCollins 1993.

Keay, John: *India: A History*, HarperCollins 2001.

Keay, John: *The Spice Route*, John Murray 2005.

Khilnani, Sunil: *The Idea of India*, Hamish Hamilton 1997.

Little, J. H.: 'The Black Hole – The Question of Holwell's Veracity', *Bengal: Past and Present*, XII (1916).

MacFarlane, Iris: *Black Hole: The Making of a Legend*, Allen and Unwin 1975.

Markovitz, Claude (ed.): *History of Modern India 1480–1950*, Anthem 2002.

Marshall, P. J.: *Bengal: The British Bridgehead: Eastern India 1740–1828*, New Cambridge History of India, Cambridge University Press 1988.

Marshall, P. J.: *Trade and Conquest: Studies on the Rise of British Domination in India*, Variorum 1993.

Marshall, P. J.: *The Oxford History of the British Empire*, vol. 2: *The Eighteenth Century*, Oxford University Press 1998.

Marshall, P. J.: *The Eighteenth Century in Indian History: Revolution or Evolution?*, Oxford University Press India 2003.

Marshall, P. J.: *The Making and Unmaking of Empires: Britain, India, and America c.1750–1783*, Oxford University Press 2005.

Mill, James: *A History of British India*, vol. 3, 4th edition, 1840.

Moorhouse, Geoffrey: *Calcutta*, Weidenfeld and Nicolson 1971.

Orme, Robert: *History of the Military Transactions of the British Nation in Indostan*, vol. 1, 1763.

Roy, Atul Chandra: *History of Bengal*, Calcutta 1986.

Stewart, Charles: *History of Bengal*, London 1813.

Twain, Mark: *Following the Equator: Journey round the World*, Dover 1989.

Wild, Antony: *The East India Company: Trade and Conquest from 1600*, HarperCollins 2000.

Index

Mullick, Raja Rajendro 196
Mumbai *see* Bombay
Mumtaz Mahal 49
Munro, T. R. 209
Murgihatta church, Calcutta 2
Murshid Kuli Khan 101
Murshidabad 47, 50, 101, 105, 174
Mutakhareen, Seer 14, 112

narcotics 23
nutmeg 22–6

Ochterlony, Sir David 20
Ochterlony's monument, Calcutta
    20
O'Hara, John 118, 120, 143
Omichand 78–9, 109–10, 121–2,
    127, 148 and *passim*
opium 23
Orme, Robert 102, 111, 146, 170,
    187

pamphlets 10
Park, The, Calcutta 124, 168
Peakes, Paul 146
pepper 23, 35–6
Perrin's Redoubt 124, 130, 133
Philip II of Spain 31
Piccard, Ensign 124, 127, 133
pirates 31, 82
Pitt, Thomas ('Diamond Pitt')
    74–7, 193
Pitt, William 193
Pitt diamond (Regence) 75–7
Plassey, battle of 19, 104, 188, 195
Pondicherry 112
Pope, Alexander 76
Portuguese
    domination of trade 29, 33, 37

missionaries 39
settlement of Goa 1, 2
press gangs 83–4
privateers 31, 35
pukka 56, 62
Pynchon, Thomas 204

Raj *see* British Empire
    employees of *see* Indian Civil
        Service
Ralegh, Sir Walter 31
Ray, Nisith 52
Renault, Colonel 113
Rocco, Fiammetta 203
Roe, Sir Thomas 38
Russell, Lady Elizabeth 17, 131,
    180

St Anne's church, Calcutta 1, 61,
    64, 95
St Jacques, marquis de 115, 126
St John's church, Calcutta 20, 64,
    213
St Nazareth, Calcutta *see*
    Armenian church
saltpetre 50
San Thome 41
Scott, Captain Caroline 95
Scott, Samuel 59, 83
Scrafton, Roger 106
Serampore 108
Seth family 53, 78, 102, 114
Seven Years War 110
Shah Jehan *see* Jehan
Shushtari, Abdul Lateef 193
Siraj-ud-daulah, nawab of Bengal
    xii, xiii, 4, 9, 19, 81, 103–6,
    107–8, 111–15, 128 and
    passim

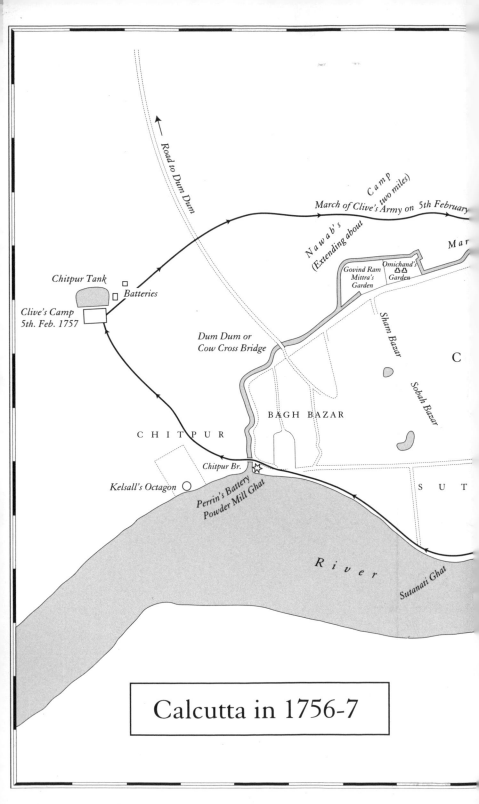

Road to Dum Dum

Camp

March of Clive's Army on 5th February

Nawab's
(Extending about two miles)

Mar

Govind Ram
Mittra's
Garden

Omichand's
Garden

Chitpur Tank

Batteries

Sham Bazar

Clive's Camp
5th. Feb. 1757

Dum Dum or
Cow Cross Bridge

C

Sobah Bazar

BAGH BAZAR

CHITPUR

Chitpur Br.

Kelsall's Octagon

Perrin's Battery
Powder Mill Ghat

SUT

River

Sutanati Ghat

Calcutta in 1756-7